# Christianity in Close-up

Key Stage 3 RE
The Christian Church

BOOK 2

Wendy Faris
Heather Hamilton

Colourpoint
Educational

ISBN: 978 1 904242 76 5

First Edition
Second Impression 2009

Layout and design: Colourpoint Books
Printed by: GPS Colour Graphics Ltd

The acknowledgements on page 102 constitute an extension of this copyright page.

**Wendy Faris** BEd MSc teaches Religious Education to A2 level. In 2006 she was awarded a fellowship from the Farmington Trust (Ernst Cook fellow).

**Heather Hamilton** BEd also teaches Religious Education to A2 level. She is Head of Religious Education in Omagh Academy, County Tyrone, and has been teaching for 11 years.

**Colourpoint Books**
Colourpoint House
Jubilee Business Park
21 Jubilee Road
Newtownards
Co Down
BT23 4YH

Tel: 028 9182 6339
Fax: 028 9182 1900
Email: info@colourpoint.co.uk
Website: www.colourpoint.co.uk

# Contents



## GUIDE TO ICONS

Activity

Discussion

Questions

Thinking exercise

## SKILLS AND CAPABILITIES KEY

***Cross-curricular Skills, and Thinking Skills and Personal Capabilities***

- **Com** Communication
- **ICT** Using ICT
- **Ma** Using Mathematics
- **MI** Managing Information
- **BC** Being Creative
- **TPD** Thinking, Problem-Solving and Decision-Making
- **SM** Self-Management
- **WO** Working with Others

***Learning for Life and Work***

- **EfE** Education for Employability
- **Cit** Local and Global Citizenship
- **PD** Personal Development

# The early Church

TPD Cit

**What is the Church?**

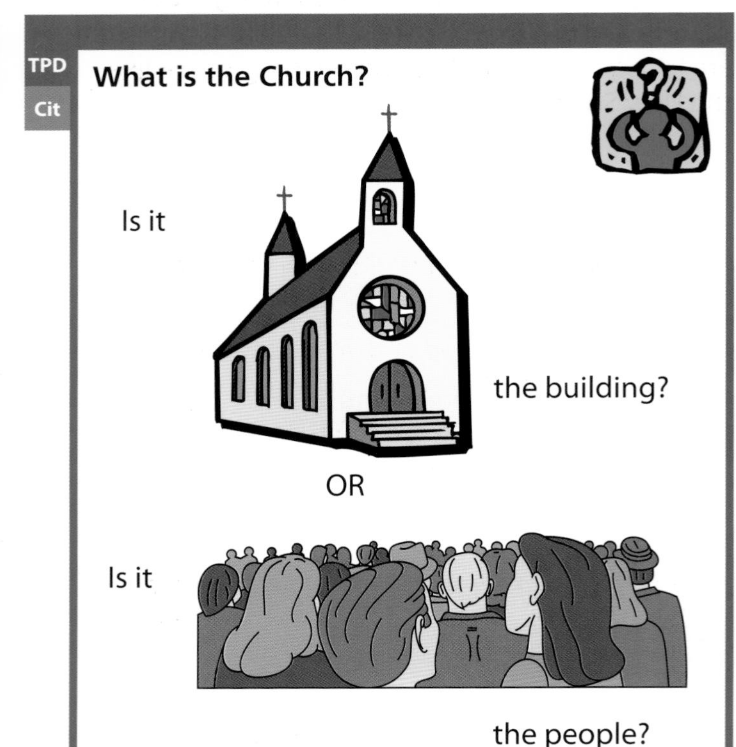


If you go to, or have ever been to, a church or another place of religious worship, how would you describe it to someone who asked?

The Christian Church began almost 2,000 years ago, on the day of **Pentecost**.

At his **Ascension** Jesus promised the disciples the gift of the **Holy Spirit**. The Holy Spirit arrived 50 days later, when the disciples were celebrating the harvest festival of Pentecost.

This event is known as the birthday of the Church because after this the Church really began to grow.

You will learn more about Pentecost on page 7.

TPD

Read Acts 2. What does this make you think?

Com BC TPD WO

In groups set up your own secret society or club.

You need to think about and discuss:

- The purpose of your club and its main aims
- Rules for membership
- A name and symbol for your club

When you have finished, talk about what was easy to decide and what was more difficult.

## The Holy Spirit

Com BC TPD WO

**The Holy Who?**

Do you think spirits exist? Why, or why not?

What do you think a spirit is?

If you could see one, what would you expect it to look like?

In fact, we can't describe what the **Holy Spirit** looks like, because we can't see it – it is a *spirit*.

However, the Bible gets over the problem by using symbols to describe it.

Cit

Here are some symbols you might see around you. Can you identify them?

Com
BC

Design a symbol that you think could represent your school. Your symbol should sum up what school means to you. Try not to use words.

It is easy to draw a symbol for something that we can see, but it is much more difficult if the thing you are trying to represent has no physical form – like the Holy Spirit.

**Here are some symbols showing what many Christians believe about the Holy Spirit.**

| | | |
|---|---|---|
| Fire gives light ... |  | The Holy Spirit shows people how to live in a dark world. |
| You can curl up in front of a fire on a cold day ... | | The Holy Spirit gives comfort during hard times. |
| Water cleans and refreshes ... |  | The Holy Spirit enters a person's life and cleans them when they believe in Jesus. |
| Wind is invisible ... |  | You cannot see the Holy Spirit, just what it does. |
| The wind is powerful ... | | The Holy Spirit has more power than people can understand. |
| A dove is gentle ... |  | The Holy Spirit deals gently with people. |
| A dove is the symbol of peace ... | | The Holy Spirit gives peace of mind. |

MI
BC
TPD

Design your own symbol for the Holy Spirit.

Write a paragraph to explain your design.

Why do you think yours is a good symbol for the Holy Spirit?

# The Trinity

The **Holy Spirit** is part of the **Trinity**. There are three parts to the Trinity – God the Father, Son and Holy Spirit – three parts, yet one God. Think about it like this:

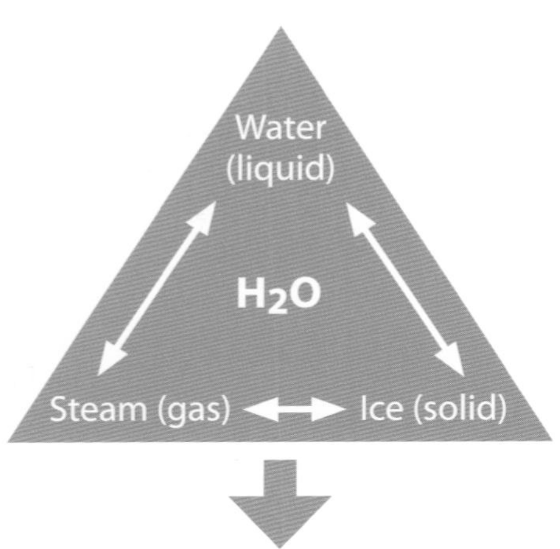


Three different forms of water, but they are all $H_2O$

*The Father – the God beyond who created the world*

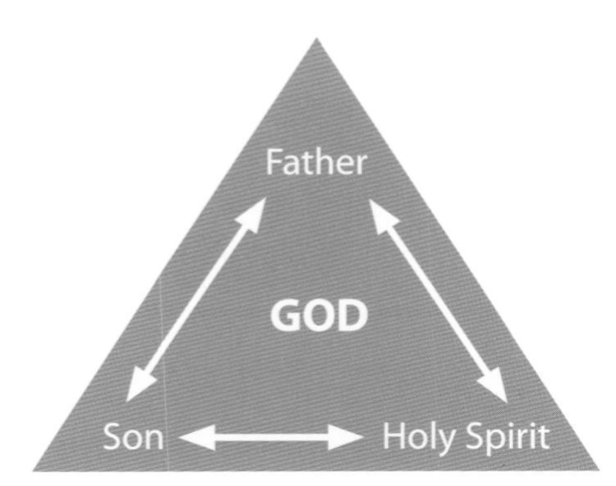


*The Son – the personal God who came to Earth and lived a human life*

*The Spirit – the God all around who helps Christians everyday*

Three different forms of God, but they are all God

Com
MI
BC
TPD
WO

Can you think of any other examples to describe the Trinity?

Which do you think is the best example and why?

A modern tapestry of the Trinity by John Piper, at the altar in Chichester Cathedral

Com
TPD
WO

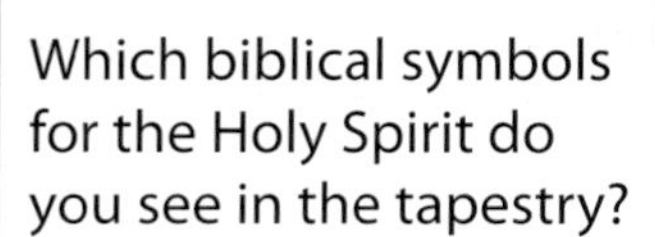

Look at the tapestry on the left.

Which biblical symbols for the Holy Spirit do you see in the tapestry?

Why do you think the designer included the images of the cross and the sun?

Which images do you think reflect God the Father?

Do you think this tapestry helps people to understand the Trinity better?

# Pentecost – the coming of the Holy Spirit

Com MI TPD SM Cit

Find out what a pilgrim is.

Today members of many faiths still go on **pilgrimages**, eg the Christian, Buddhist, Muslim and Jewish faiths.

Pick one faith and research pilgrimages made by its followers.

You could use your research to make a short presentation to your class.

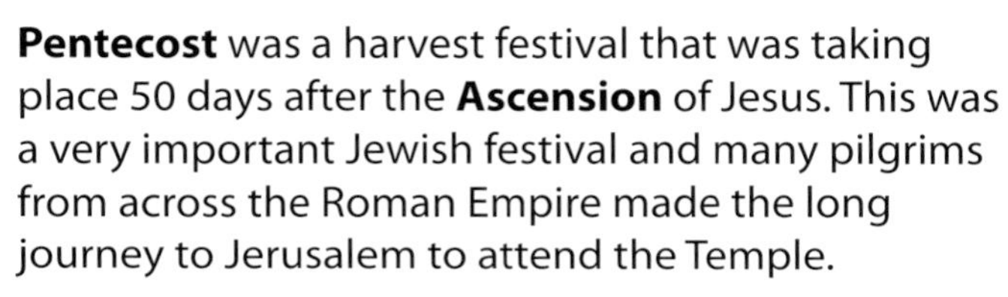

**Pentecost** was a harvest festival that was taking place 50 days after the **Ascension** of Jesus. This was a very important Jewish festival and many pilgrims from across the Roman Empire made the long journey to Jerusalem to attend the Temple.

The **apostles** were in Jerusalem, in an upstairs room. They were afraid to go outside in case people knew they were supporters of Jesus and arrested them.

This was when the **Holy Spirit** came to them.

Com WO

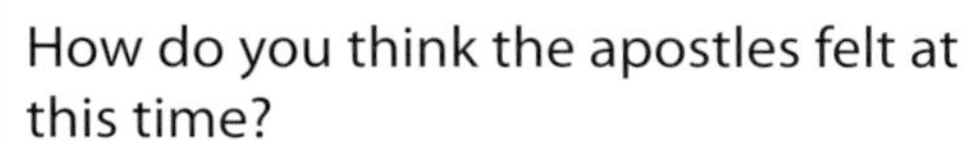

The picture above shows how someone imagined Pentecost.

How do you think the apostles felt at this time?

Com MI TPD

Write a paragraph to explain why the coming of the Holy Spirit at this particular time was good for the spread of Christianity.

(clue – pilgrims)

TPD PD

Now read the story of what happened in Acts 2 again, especially v 1–15 and v 38–47.

Why do you think there were Jews from so many different countries in Jerusalem at the time?

Would you be willing to travel hundreds of miles for anything?

Com MI BC TPD SM

Read some newspaper articles. Then think about the following questions and make a list:

- What makes a good article?
- What should it include?

Now write your own article on the events of Pentecost. Make sure it includes all the features on your list.

BC TPD

Design a birthday card to celebrate Pentecost as the birthday of the Church.

# Prejudice and discrimination

TPD
Cit
PD

Sometimes the way we see people affects the way we treat them.

Look at the photographs below and, without thinking too much, write down the first five words that come to mind for each one.

Now look at the photographs again and ask yourself:

Why do you think those words came to mind?

Would you change your mind about any of them now? Why, or why not?

©iStockphoto.com/track5

©iStockphoto.com/olandesina

©iStockphoto.com/Ravet007

**Discrimination** is an *action*. It means treating someone unfairly because of your prejudice. For example, *"I won't employ him because he is a different religion to me."*

**Prejudice** is an *attitude*. It means having an opinion that is not based on fact. For example, *"I think he is a troublemaker because he wears a hoodie."*

BC
TPD
Cit

Draw two columns with the headings 'Prejudice' and 'Discrimination'.

Decide whether each statement is an example of *prejudice* or of *discrimination* and write it in the correct column. Then try to think of more statements to put in each column.

I think Polish people should be sent back to Poland because they take our jobs.

I won't offer her the job because she has a disability.

Homeless people are only in that situation because they won't help themselves.

All women are bad drivers.

In the United Kingdom (UK), gay people weren't allowed to join the army until 2000.

All teenagers are troublemakers.

The Indian family had to leave their home because of racist attacks and abuse.

I won't get on a plane if I see any Arabs getting onto it.

# Persecution of the Church

Com
MI
WO
Cit

What is persecution?

Can you think of examples happening today?

Try to think of local examples as well as examples from around the world.

The Christians were a **minority** following a new religion. Because of this many people were suspicious of them.

The prejudice against the Christians came from two main sources:

1. The Jews – they disagreed with the Christian idea that Jesus was the **Messiah**. They also objected to Christians allowing **Gentiles** into their meetings.
2. The Romans – Christians wouldn't worship Roman gods and the Romans felt that the gods were angry because of this and that disasters would happen.

For these reasons, both groups persecuted the Christians.

## THE JEWISH PERSECUTION

Com
TPD
WO
Cit

What is a martyr?

Can you think of any modern examples of people who are thought of as martyrs?

Why might people disagree about whether or not someone is a martyr?

### *The death of Stephen – the first Christian martyr*

Stephen was a **deacon** at the beginning of the Church in Jerusalem. He was a very good speaker and was popular with the people, but he also had many opponents amongst the Jews. They started arguments with Stephen in the hope that he would say something they could use against him, but Stephen always spoke wisely.

The Jews then persuaded some men to claim that Stephen had **blasphemed** against God. Stephen was arrested and brought before the **Sanhedrin** for trial.

In his answer at this trial Stephen criticised the Jewish priests. He also questioned the Jewish idea that God lived in the **Holy of Holies** in the Temple by saying that God *"does not live in houses made by men"* (Acts 7:48).

This made the Jews angry and they ordered people to drag Stephen out of the city and stone him. As they stoned him Stephen prayed that God would forgive them for what they were doing.

*Stephen being stoned*

Stephen became the first Christian martyr – the first person to die because he was a Christian.

You can read more about Stephen in Acts 6–8.

Com
MI
TPD
SM
WO

**Priority pyramid**

Working with a partner, draw a pyramid and give it the title 'Things that make Stephen memorable and important'.

Fill in your pyramid, putting the things which you think are the most important at the top and the least important at the bottom.

You could then report back to the rest of the class, explaining your choices.

# THE ROMAN PERSECUTION

For years the Romans persecuted the followers of Christ. Many Christians died for their faith – they became martyrs.

The first Roman Emperor to persecute the Christian Church was called Nero.

In AD 64 a great fire broke out in Rome and much of the city was destroyed. The residents of the city called for those responsible to be caught.

Many people think that Nero planned the fire himself because he wanted to build a new and more modern city as a symbol of his power. However, when he saw the public's reaction he became afraid of people beginning to suspect his involvement. He looked around for someone to blame and the Christians became his scapegoat.

MI
PD

What is a scapegoat?

Can you find out where the word comes from?

Can you think of examples of people being used as scapegoats?

Have you ever been used as a scapegoat?

The answer to this question is quite simple – many of the Romans already hated and feared the Christians.

There were a number of reasons for this:

1. The Christians met in secret and their meetings were open only to Christians. This made the Romans suspect the Christians of plotting against the Empire.
2. Loyalty to the Emperor was very important in Rome. Every Roman citizen was expected to burn incense to the Emperor as a symbol of this loyalty. Christians would not do this, because it broke one of the **Ten Commandments**: *"You shall have no other gods before me"* (Deuteronomy 5:7). So the Romans thought that Christians were disloyal to the State.
3. The Romans heard that Christians ate the body and blood of Christ. They did not realise that, to these Christians, bread and wine were *symbols* of the body and blood of Christ. The Romans accused the Christians of cannibalism – they thought that they ate their own children!
4. The Christians refused to make an idol to their God so the Romans accused them of **atheism,** which means not believing in any god at all.
5. The Romans worshipped **pagan** gods and they believed that when the gods were happy the Roman Empire did well. However, if people did not worship the gods the Romans believed they would become angry and bad things would happen to the Empire (eg floods, invasions, famine). When these things happened some Romans blamed the Christians for making the gods angry.
6. Christians did not believe in violence and some of them would not join the army. The Romans saw this as a lack of loyalty to the Empire and this made them suspicious of the Christians.
7. Christians referred to each other as brothers and sisters in Christ. When the Romans heard that Christian brothers and sisters were getting married, they misunderstood this and thought that *real* brothers and sisters were getting married!

So really the Romans hated the Christians because they did not understand them and had confused ideas about Christian practices.

### *How Nero persecuted the Christian Church*

Nero killed thousands of Christians in many horrible ways:

1. Christians of all ages were thrown to the lions and wild dogs in the **arena**.
2. Christians were sewn into the skins of wild beasts and were attacked by dogs.
3. Some Christians were crucified.
4. Christians were burned alive. Nero had Christians tied to posts in his garden, where pitch and tar were poured over them and they were set alight. They burned as human torches and Nero ran his chariot races through a lane of burning men and women.

Two famous Christians who are believed to have been martyred during Nero's reign are Peter and Paul. Because he was a Roman citizen, Paul was beheaded instead of being crucified like Peter. Tradition says that Peter asked to be crucified upside down.

TPD

Why do you think Peter asked to be crucified upside down?

MI
TPD

1 What is a martyr?

2 Who was the first Roman Emperor to persecute the Christian Church?

3 When did this persecution begin?

4 Explain why Nero began to persecute the Church?

5 Why did many Romans already hate the Christians?

6 Outline some of the ways in which Nero persecuted the Christians.

7 Do you think there are any Christians in the world today who still suffer for their beliefs? Explain your answer.

## SECRET SIGNS AND SYMBOLS

It was very dangerous to be a Christian at this time and so the early Christians used secret signs to communicate with each other.

If you were a Christian arriving in a new town, you couldn't just go up to anyone and ask where the local Christians met for worship. Secret symbols were used to mark fellow Christians' homes, and places where they worshipped. The symbol may have been discreetly carved on the doorpost of a house or painted on a wall.

The fish was used as a symbol because the Greek word for fish *(ichthus)* spells out the Greek initials of the words 'Jesus Christ, God's Son, Saviour'.

The chi-rho was made by joining the first two letters of the Greek word for Christ.

The anchor sign was used by the early Christians in underground caves and tunnels, called catacombs, in Rome. It may have been used because it looks like a cross or because of the passage in the Bible which says, *"We have this hope as an anchor for the soul ..."* (Hebrews 6:19).

**I.N.R.I.**

The letters 'INRI' are the initials of the Latin words for 'Jesus of Nazareth, the King of the Jews'. They were the words written by Pilate and fastened to the cross on which Jesus was crucified (John 19:19).

Com
BC
TPD

Design your own secret symbol for Christians.

Write a paragraph to explain the meaning behind your design.

# An outline of Church history

EARLY HISTORY

between 3 and 5 BC – Jesus was born in Bethlehem, Judea, in what is now Israel.

about 30 AD – The Romans crucified Jesus. After his resurrection he went up to heaven and his disciples received the **Holy Spirit**. They started to preach and the Christian Church began.

about 35 AD – Saul became a Christian on the road to Damascus. His name was changed to Paul, and he began to preach the message of Christianity and set up churches.

64 AD – The Emperor Nero began to persecute the Christian Church.

597 AD – Augustine brought Christianity to England. Some think that the Roman soldiers posted there had already brought Christianity to Britain.

1054 AD – The Church split because of different teachings. Two separate groups were formed – the Catholic Church and the Orthodox Church.

CONFLICT

1517 AD – Martin Luther wrote his '95 **Theses**' and is said to have nailed them to the door of the Castle Church in Wittenberg, Germany. He then split from the Catholic Church and the **Protestant** movement began.

1534 AD – Henry VIII made himself head of the Church in England, broke ties with the Catholic Church and set up the **Anglican** Church.

1500s – The Presbyterian Church was founded by John Knox.

CHANGE

late 1500s/ early 1600s – The Congregational Church was formed.

early 1600s – The Baptist Church was formed by Thomas Helwys, among others.

mid 1600s – George Fox founded the Religious Society of Friends (Quakers).

early 1700s – John and Charles Wesley founded the Methodist Church.

1878 AD – The Christian Mission (founded by William Booth in 1865) became the **Salvation** Army.

At first all Christians belonged to one organisation, but over 2,000 years they have broken into many different groups. Each of these groups practises Christianity in a slightly different way.

MI TPD

Before you study any more, write down two reasons why you think Christians have split into different groups.

# The modern Church

There are many denominations within Christianity, but they all believe in the **Trinity** and that Jesus was the Son of God. The differences between them are found in some of their other beliefs and practices.

MI

What is a denomination?

Try to list as many different denominations within Christianity as you can.

Now do some research to see if there are any you've never heard of.

## THE CATHOLIC CHURCH

The Catholic Church is based in Rome and is led by the **Pope**. He is the spiritual leader of the Church and is responsible for all its rulings and teachings.

Mary, the mother of Jesus, is considered very important by the Catholic Church. Catholics pray to her, asking her to talk to Jesus for them.

*A statue of Mary*

## PROTESTANT CHURCHES

There are many different denominations within the **Protestant** tradition.

These groups share the same main beliefs but they may think differently about some things, and their Sunday services may be different.

The Protestant Churches do not recognise the authority of the Pope. They have their own religious leaders instead, for example:

Church of Ireland – **Archbishop**
Presbyterian – Moderator
Baptist – President
Methodist – President

MI

Find out who are the leaders of the main Protestant Churches today.

Com MI TPD WO Cit

What things are the same between different Christian denominations?

What things are different?

What do you think are the most important similarities and differences?

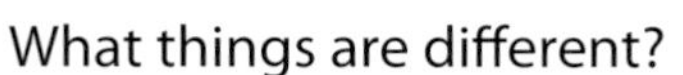

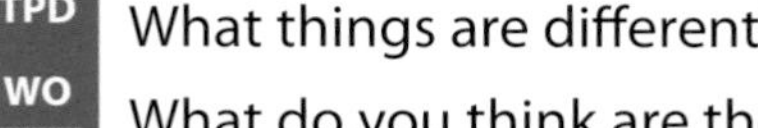

## ECUMENISM

The **ecumenical** movement believes that Churches should become more united. It encourages Christians to work together and forget their differences. Some Christians are in favour of this and some are against it.

Com TPD WO Cit

Do you think all Christians should worship together in the one Church?

Are there any things which would make this difficult?

Can you think of anything good about doing this?

MI Cit

**Web search**

Find out about Corrymeela.
Look up its website (www.corrymeela.org) and write down:

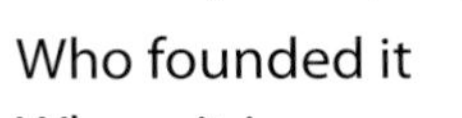

Who founded it
Where it is
What kind of work it does

# HOW CHRISTIANS WORSHIP AND EXPRESS THEIR FAITH

MI

Read the following Bible passages and write down some of the activities that were happening within the early Church.

| | | |
|---|---|---|
| Acts 2:38 | Acts 2:44–45 | 1 Corinthians 11:26 |
| Acts 2:41 | Acts 2:47 | 1 Timothy 2:8 |

MI

Read the church notices below and list some of the activities that are taking place in the twenty-first century Church. Did any of these activities take place in the early Church? Place a tick beside any that did.

**Youth Outreach Event**

You are warmly invited to an evening of praise and fellowship at First Presbyterian Church, Moneydew.

Special guest speakers and singers

Offering in aid of Youth Evangelism

**BOND STREET METHODIST CHURCH**

Sunday 13th February

10.15 am Meeting for Prayer

11.00 am Revd P Canning

Sacrament of Baptism

Crèche & Children's Church

7.00 pm Praise Evening

**Barker Street Gospel Hall**

Missionary Report Meeting

Thursday 8 pm

Mr and Mrs D Spence will report on their work in Botswana.

***Holy Trinity Parish Church***

*Celebration of First Communion*

*Officiating – Fr. E Connor*

*Service commences at 11 am*

***Elim Pentecostal Church***
***Berkley Avenue***

*Gives you a warm invitation to our service*

*Sunday at 11 am - Worship, Ministry, Communion*
*7 pm - Gospel Service*
*Singing by the Junior Choir*

***Burn Baptist Church***

***Sunday Services:***

*11 am and 7 pm, preceded by prayer at 10.30 and 6.30*

*11 am – Ministry and the Lord's Table*

*7 pm – Guest Service; singer: J Harris testimony: E Crawford*

*Mid-week Prayer Meeting – Tuesday at 8 pm*

Com
MI
BC
TPD

Design a poster advertising some of the activities taking place in the early Church.

## CHURCH ATTENDANCE

Com
ICT
Ma
MI
BC
TPD
WO
Cit

Conduct and compile a survey of 20 people on church attendance.

This can be done in groups of four, with each member of your group asking five people the questions in the survey.

Think of questions like these:

Do you attend church?

If so, how often do you attend?

Why do you/do you not attend church?

Present your results in a graph using Microsoft® Excel and report back to the rest of the class.

Use the results to work out whether church attendance is still important to people.

If it is, what are the reasons why it is?

If it isn't, what are the reasons why it isn't?

What do you think of the reasons people gave for attending or not attending church?

Com
BC
TPD
WO

**The ideal church**

Many people don't feel that there is anything for them at church.

Divide into groups and discuss the following questions:

What do you think church should be like?

What sorts of things should a church be involved in?

What do you think should happen during a church service?

Staying in your groups, now plan a church service. You will need to decide:

The order in which things happen

A theme

The music you will have

The prayers

The readings

What the talk or sermon will be about

Compare your service with those of other groups. Are there differences?

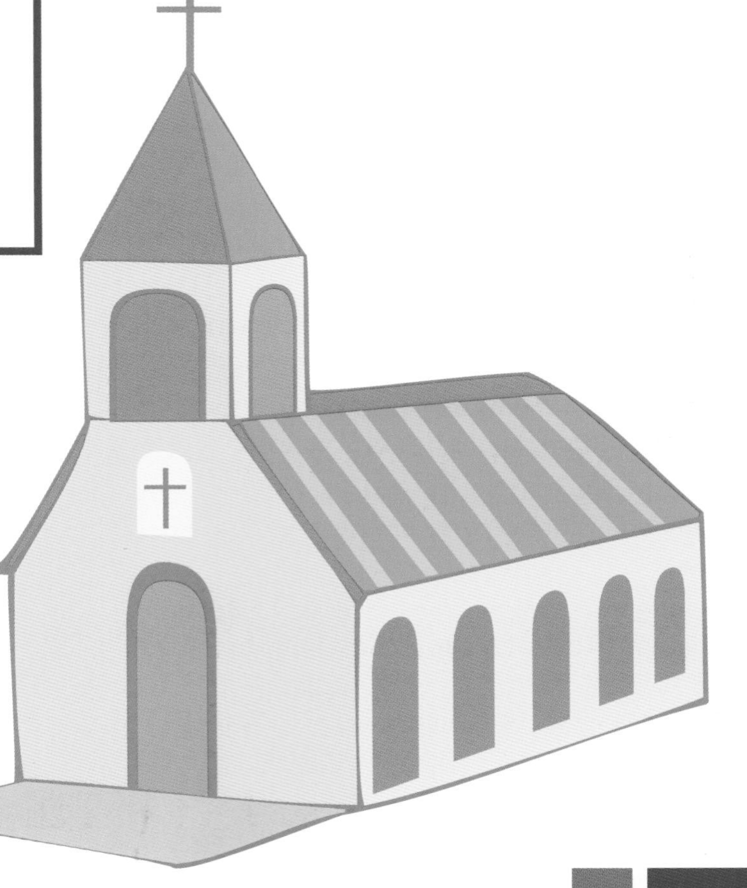

# The Church through the ages

## The Celtic Church

### Saint Patrick (fifth century AD)

MI

Find out:

What kind of religion existed in Ireland at this time?

What gods did the people worship?

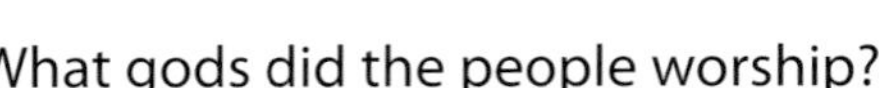

#### PATRICK'S EARLY LIFE

Very little is known for certain about Patrick, the patron saint of Ireland.

He was born in Roman Britain, probably near the beginning of the fifth century AD (the 400s).

His full name was Magonus Succatus Patricius.

Patrick's father was called Calpurnius and he was a very rich man. We know this because he owned a villa with servants.

Life for the young Patrick would have been very comfortable. Calpurnius was an important official in their home town of Bannavem Taburniae.

At this time, priests could get married. Patrick's grandfather was called Potitus. He was a leader or priest in the Christian Church in the area.

In spite of this, Patrick later wrote that when he was young he *"did not, indeed, know the true God"*.

Patrick does not mention his mother in his writings but later tradition names her as Concessa.

When Patrick was about 16 years old, some armed men raided his home town on the west coast of Britain.

They were Irish raiders who had sailed to Britain to find plunder. They also captured people to use as slaves.

Patrick was captured and taken to pre-Christian Ireland where he was sold as a slave.

In later life Patrick described the raid in the *Confession* (one of Patrick's writings which you will read more about later). This is what he said:

*I was at that time about sixteen years of age. I did not, indeed, know the true God; and I was taken into captivity in Ireland with many thousands of people, according to our deserts, for quite drawn away from God, we did not keep his precepts, nor were we obedient to our priests ...*

MI

Why did Patrick believe that he deserved to be captured and taken to Ireland?

Patrick's education was cut short when he was captured and brought to Ireland. Because of this, he may not have learnt the official language (Latin) properly and he later said he couldn't write well in Latin.

Com
MI

Write a summary of Patrick's early life. Make sure you mention:

- His possible date of birth
- His family life (make sure you note all the important people)
- Religion
- Education
- The raid on his home

Com
MI
BC
TPD
WO

Make a list of words that you think sum up how Patrick was feeling at this time in his life.

Now divide into groups and put together a short news item for Bannavem Radio. Report on the raid and how it affected people, especially Patrick's family.

Remember to interview the key people.

## IRELAND BEFORE PATRICK

Com
TPD

How would you describe Ireland nowadays to someone who had never been there?

### *People*

The Ireland that Patrick came to was very different to Ireland today. Patrick came to an island divided into many small **kingdoms**. These kingdoms were ruled by **local kings** or **chieftains**.

There were about 150 rulers at this time. Each one ruled over his own kingdom.

### *Environment*

Patrick came from Roman Britain where families like his enjoyed roads, central heating, stone buildings, baths, paved floors, plumbing and many other comforts.

He was brought to Ireland where the people were living in much more **primitive** conditions.

*A druid ceremony*

### *Religion*

At this time in Ireland most people were **pagan**.

They worshipped nature – the sun, rivers, and trees. They also believed in magic and witchcraft and had great respect for the **druids**.

The druids were the priests of the time and they had a great deal of power over the people.

Animal and possibly even human **sacrifices** were part of pagan worship in Ireland at this time.

BC
PD

Look at the picture above.

If you came across this group of people in a forest, how would you feel?

If you could talk to one of the people in the group, what questions would you ask?

## PATRICK'S LIFE IN IRELAND

It is thought that Patrick was sold to a local chieftain called Miliucc and he spent the next six years of his life as a shepherd.

There is a tradition that Patrick was a slave on Slemish Mountain in County Antrim. However, Patrick does not mention Slemish in his writings. Instead he says he dreamt of voices calling him from *"beside the forest of Foclut, which is near the western sea"*.

It is believed that this forest was in the west of Ireland, possibly in present-day County Mayo near the town of Killala.

This is the only place that Patrick mentions in his writings. He says nothing about Tara, Slemish, Armagh or Downpatrick, even though these places are often associated with him.

Patrick spent his days and nights on the hillside looking after Miliucc's sheep.

Conditions were hard and in his writings Patrick recalls how he was hungry and cold and at times felt ready to collapse.

Patrick's plight moved him to turn to God and he became a Christian.

## PATRICK'S ESCAPE FROM IRELAND

In the *Confession*, Patrick describes how he escaped from Ireland.

One night he had a dream in which he was told a boat was waiting to take him home to Britain. In the dream he heard the words, *"Behold, your ship is ready."*

Patrick believed this was God speaking to him and he knew he had to travel south to find this ship.

He travelled 200 miles, possibly to Wexford, where a boat heading for Britain was waiting.

But when Patrick spoke to the captain, he refused to allow Patrick onto the boat. Patrick turned away and prayed for God's guidance. Before he had finished praying he heard a crew member calling to him.

They had changed their minds and were prepared to take him on board.

Patrick was 22 years old at the time.

MI

1 How was Ireland ruled at this time?
2 Describe the religion practised in Ireland at this time.
3 Who was thought to be Patrick's master in Ireland?
4 Where did Patrick spend his captivity? Explain fully.
5 Why did Patrick become a Christian? What do you think of his reasons?
6 Explain how Patrick escaped from Ireland.

Ma

A B C D E F G H I J K L M N O P Q
R S T U V W X Y Z

Add or subtract the number of letters to work out the coded message.

N+2 B–1 Q+3 T–2 H+1 A+2 M–2
Z–3 D–3 P+3
E–3 P+2 N+1 X–3 F+1 F+2 P+4
R+2 P–1
H+1 N+4 A+4 M–1 F–5 P–2 A+3
D–3 T–1 C–2
V–3 J+2 G–6 R+4 C+2.

U–1 P+2 D–3 F–2 J–1 R+2 M–4 M+2 I+5
P+3 P+4 D–3 R+2 C+2 K+8
W–3 K–3 F–5 P+4 M–5 E+4 P+3
A+2 D–4 O+1 R+2 J–1 Z–4 K–2 R+2 S+6
U+2 D–3 P+3
R+1 N+2 H–3 K+3 R+2 M+2 I+5
U–2 J+2 G–2 J+3 F+3 Q+2 M–5.

## THE CALL TO BE A MISSIONARY

Some time after Patrick had escaped from **slavery** and made his way home to Britain, he had a dream.

In the dream a messenger called Victoricus arrived from Ireland with many letters, and handed one of these to Patrick.

As Patrick began to read the letter in his dream, it was as if he heard voices from Ireland calling to him saying, *"We beg you, holy youth, that you shall come and shall walk again among us."*

Patrick became sure that this was God calling him to become a missionary in Ireland. He spent a number of years studying and making up for the interruption in his education when he had been captured.

During this time the Church in Rome decided that someone should be sent to Ireland. A monk called Palladius was chosen to go. The **Pope** said he was to go to the Irish people who believed in Christ.

Palladius was sent to Ireland in AD 431 and this is the only date that we can be certain of in the whole story of Patrick.

Palladius died a year or two later, and it was the Church in Britain that asked Patrick to lead another mission to Ireland.

## THE WORK BEGINS

People believe that Patrick and his helpers may have landed their boat near Strangford Lough in County Down.

They were immediately spotted by a swineherd, who ran to tell his master Dichu about these strange people.

When Dichu was told that a group of strange men had landed, he came at once and set his dog at them. Legend says that Patrick prayed and the dog became quiet and friendly.

Dichu was impressed with Patrick and listened to his preaching. He became a Christian and is traditionally thought of as Patrick's first Irish **convert**.

To show his gratitude, Dichu gave Patrick a barn at Saul, near Downpatrick, to use as his first church in Ireland (*Saul* is Irish for 'barn').

In AD 445, it is said Patrick built his first church in Ireland. It was in Armagh and was made of stone.

The present Church of Ireland cathedral is the successor to this first church.

*Armagh cathedral today*

Patrick faced many problems during his mission. The druids saw him as a threat and a rival and tried to have him killed on many occasions.

TPD

Why did the druids hate Patrick so much? What were they afraid of?

## PATRICK AND LAOGHAIRE

At springtime, the pagans met to honour the sun.

A very important king, Laoghaire (pronounced *Leary*), had ordered that nobody else could light a fire until he had lit a special **sacred** fire to honour the sun.

However, because it was the Christian Easter, Patrick and his followers lit a fire to celebrate Jesus as the light of the world.

Laoghaire was furious when he saw the fire – he thought that someone was defying him. He went with his soldiers to Slane Hill, the site of Patrick's fire, to kill the offenders.

Patrick told the king who they were and explained that they only wanted to spread the **gospel**.

The king calmed down and he asked them to come to his court at Tara the next day.

*This is what one artist thought Patrick's procession to Tara might have looked like.*

Com
BC
TPD
WO

Look at the picture on the left.

Who do you see?

What things are they carrying?

Why do you think they are carrying them?

This picture was painted hundreds of years after the event. Do *you* think this is what it would have looked like?

**The shamrock**

Father
Son
Holy Spirit

Although the legend of the shamrock is associated with Patrick, it comes from very much later – possibly even as late as the seventeenth century (1600s).

The legend says that Patrick used the shamrock to explain the **Trinity** to Laoghaire – three leaves yet one plant, three parts to God yet one God.

Legend says that the druids were angry at Patrick and tried to trap him by asking if he could make snow. Patrick said that it was God who made the weather, not him.

However, just at that moment it began to snow. Patrick made the sign of the cross and the snow immediately disappeared.

After this contest of power between Patrick and the druids, Patrick preached to the king.

Some sources say the king was converted to Christianity, but other sources tell us that he wasn't because he believed he would be betraying his ancestors who had trusted him with the land and its traditions.

However, the most important thing is that he said he wouldn't stop Patrick from preaching his religion.

You can read an extract from a hymn associated with Patrick below.

**The Breastplate of Saint Patrick**

*Christ be with me,*
*Christ within me.*
*Christ behind me,*
*Christ before me,*
*Christ beside me.*
*Christ to win me.*
*Christ to comfort*
*and restore me.*
*Christ beneath me,*
*Christ above me.*
*Christ in quiet,*
*Christ in danger.*
*Christ in hearts of*
*all that love me.*
*Christ in mouth of*
*friend and stranger.*

TPD

Can you think why these words were called 'The Breastplate of Saint Patrick'?

Com
MI
TPD

1 Write a detailed account of Patrick's call to Ireland as a missionary.
2 When do historians think Patrick may have come to Ireland as a missionary?
3 Where does tradition say Patrick landed in Ireland?
4 Imagine you are Dichu. Why would you be wary of Patrick at first? Why do you change your mind?
5 Who was the important king that Patrick confronted?
6 Why was this king angry with Patrick?
7 Why was the support of this king so important?
8 Why is the shamrock used to explain the Trinity? Do you think it is a good illustration?

## THE LEGENDS

The earliest book in which we have records of what was remembered about Patrick is known as the *Book of Armagh*. It is thought to have been put together in the early ninth century by a scribe named Ferdomnach, and contains important early texts about Patrick. We are told that what was recorded there was written *"to the honour and praise of the Lord and in beloved memory of Patrick".*

However, a lot of time had passed after Patrick's death before the first accounts of his life were written. The memory of the kind of person he was had faded, so in order to honour him the people who wrote about him claimed he performed amazing miracles.

Instead of the humble writer of the *Confession*, the legends tell of a wonder-worker who put curses on those who opposed him.

It is possible that another reason for making up these legends was to help Christianity compete with paganism. Pagan people were superstitious and believed in the magical powers of the druids. Therefore, the people who wrote about Patrick might have thought that these stories would make the Irish more interested in Christianity.

### *SOME OF THE LEGENDS*

#### *The snakes*

There is a legend that Patrick banished all the snakes from Ireland. It has been told so many times that not all the versions are the same.

One account says that Patrick stood on a hill and banished the snakes into the sea using his wooden staff.

However, one old snake refused to leave so Patrick played a trick on it. He made a box and told the snake to get into it. The snake insisted that the box was too small and Patrick and the snake argued. To prove that it was right and Patrick was wrong, the snake got into the box. Patrick then closed the lid, trapping the snake in the box, and threw it into the sea.

Some people think that the story of Patrick and the snakes is meant to symbolise how he banished paganism from Ireland and replaced it with Christianity.

#### *Miliucc*

It is said that soon after Patrick returned to Ireland he wanted to see his old master and if possible convert him to Christianity.

Miliucc had heard of Patrick's arrival and his supposed powers and was afraid he had returned to get revenge. Miliucc gathered together all his possessions, went into his house and set it alight, killing himself.

#### *Saint Benignus*

Another legend says that Patrick was travelling towards Tara when he lay down to rest and fell asleep. As he slept, a young boy came past. The boy gathered flowers and placed them on Patrick's chest.

When Patrick woke up he saw the boy and realised there was something special about him. He foretold that he would have a great future. The boy was called Benignus and he became Patrick's successor as leader of the Church in Armagh.

### The robber Bishop of Man

According to this legend, there was once a robber called Macull who terrorised the people in Saul and Downpatrick. At first he wanted to kill Patrick, but then decided to make him look foolish instead.

Macull made one of his followers pretend to be ill and then asked Patrick to heal him. Patrick knew what he was doing and told Macull he had better check his friend. When Macull investigated he discovered to his horror that his friend was dead.

Macull decided that Patrick really was a man of God and he converted to Christianity. He was sorry for what he had done. As a punishment Patrick ordered him to leave Ireland. He was put into a boat without any oars and Patrick told him he must serve God wherever the boat landed.

The legend says that he landed on the Isle of Man and later became the **Bishop** of Man.

BC

If you were Macull, what would you have thought when you saw that your friend was dead?

### The deer

The druids were jealous of Patrick and were always plotting to kill him. This legend tells of one occasion when Patrick and his friends were facing an ambush organised by the druids. Patrick turned himself and his companions into deer so that their enemies could not see them.

MI TPD

1 Who is thought to have put together the *Book of Armagh*?

2 Why would some people not be sure if they could believe the information in the *Book of Armagh*?

3 Think of at least two reasons why people made up legends about Patrick.

4 From what you have read, what is your impression of the *real* Patrick? Why do you think this?

Com MI TPD WO

Which legends do you think may have happened and why?

Which legends do you think probably didn't happen and why?

## PATRICK'S WRITINGS

We don't know what Patrick looked like, but we get an idea of the kind of man he was from his writings.

We are almost certain that Patrick wrote two things during his lifetime:

1. The *Confession*
2. The *Letter to Coroticus*

### The Confession

Patrick probably wrote the *Confession* when he was an old man.

As well as being an outline of his life, Patrick used the *Confession* as a way of defending himself against accusations that British bishops made about him and his work in Ireland. Some of them said Patrick was using his mission to make money, which he kept.

In fact, Patrick did refuse to send money from the Church in Ireland to Britain, but he did not keep it for himself. He preferred to use it for the good of the Irish Church.

The bishops also condemned Patrick because they said he wasn't well-educated. He thought of himself as a bishop in Ireland, but they felt that he was not properly qualified to be one.

Com MI BC TPD WO EfE

Find a copy of the *Confession*. If you can't find it in a book, you should be able to find one on the internet.

Once you have read it, write down anything that puzzles you, or anything that surprises you.

Then have a class discussion about the kind of man Patrick seems to be.

How important do *you* think it is to be well-educated?

Com
MI
TPD
WO

Patrick wrote in the *Confession*:

*"... I know for certain, that before I was humbled I was like a stone lying in deep mire, and he that is mighty came and in his mercy raised me up and, indeed, lifted me high up and placed me on top of the wall."*

Talk about this and decide what you think Patrick means.

TPD

Read the following extracts from the *Confession* and answer the questions.

*" I, Patrick, a sinner, a most simple countryman, the least of all the faithful and most contemptible to many, had for father the* ***deacon*** *Calpurnius, son of the late Potitus, a priest, of the settlement of Bannavem Taburniae; he had a small villa nearby where I was taken captive. I was at that time about sixteen years of age. I did not, indeed, know the true God; and I was taken into captivity in Ireland with many thousands of people, according to our deserts, for quite drawn away from God, we did not keep his precepts ...*

*And there the Lord opened my mind to an awareness of my unbelief, in order that, even so late, I might remember my transgressions and turn with all my heart to the Lord my God, who had regard for my insignificance and pitied my youth and ignorance. And he watched over me ... as a father would his son.*

*Therefore, indeed, I cannot keep silent, nor would it be proper, so many favours and graces has the Lord deigned to bestow on me in the land of my captivity ...*

*But after I reached Ireland I used to pasture the flock each day and I used to pray many times a day. More and more did the love of God, and my fear of him and faith increase, and my spirit was moved so that in a day [I said] from one up to a hundred prayers, and in the night a like number; besides I used to stay out in the forests and on the mountain and I would wake up before daylight to pray in the snow, in icy coldness, in rain, and I used to feel neither ill nor any slothfulness, because, as I now see, the Spirit was burning in me at that time."*

Use a dictionary to find out the meaning of any words that you don't understand.

1 Did Patrick consider himself to be important? Give reasons for your answer.

2 Was Patrick religious when he was young? Explain why you think this.

3 Why did Patrick think he had been taken into slavery?

4 How did Patrick spend the day when he was a slave?

### *The Letter to Coroticus*

This letter was written to a king called Coroticus who had killed many of Patrick's converts and kidnapped others. Patrick was angry with Coroticus and wrote a letter of **excommunication**, telling the people to have nothing to do with him.

Com
MI
BC
TPD
WO

Find a copy of the *Letter to Coroticus*.

Compare it to the *Confession* and discuss the following questions:

Does Patrick sound the same in each piece of writing?

What things are the same?

What do you think seems to be different?

From your study of the life of Patrick and his writings, what qualities do you think Patrick had which helped make him so successful in spreading Christianity in Ireland?

## PATRICK'S ACHIEVEMENTS

1. Patrick helped to spread Christianity in pagan Ireland. In his writings he claims that thousands of Irish men and women were converted.
2. He also says that, because of his work, many people were becoming monks and nuns.
3. According to tradition, he founded many churches in Ireland.
4. He left a record of his life and work in the *Confession*.
5. He set an example for many others to follow.

## PATRICK'S DEATH

The death and burial of Patrick is surrounded by great mystery. Tradition says he died on 17 March at Saul, but the exact year is unknown. Some think he died about 461, but others think it could have been as late as 493.

Legend says there was a bitter argument over where the body should be buried. This was settled by making two untamed bullocks pull a cart which had Patrick's coffin on it.

It was agreed that the place where they stopped should be the burial site and that a church would be built there to honour Patrick.

The site is believed to be near the present Church of Ireland cathedral in Downpatrick. A granite stone to mark the place of burial was put there in 1901, but we cannot be absolutely sure that this is where Patrick was buried.

**Remember!**

There are many legends about Patrick. Some of the stories about him were written down hundreds of years after he died.

But it is very important to remember that some things *are* known and that Patrick was a *real* person.

Hundreds and hundreds of years after his death, people still talk about him and honour him.

MI

Make a timeline for Saint Patrick. On it, note all the important dates and events in his life.

Com MI BC TPD

Draw a design for a mural to celebrate the life and work of Saint Patrick.

MI

Find out as many ways as you can that Saint Patrick is remembered today, not just in Ireland (eg festivals, parades, societies).

Com MI BC TPD

Make a wall display on Saint Patrick.

Com MI BC TPD WO

In groups, create a 'This is Your Life' drama on Saint Patrick. You will need

A presenter

Saint Patrick

Some of the people from his life.

Each of these people should make up a short outline of how they met Patrick and how he affected them.

## MONASTERIES IN IRELAND

At the time of Patrick many people were attracted to the monastic way of life.

### *Structure*

The buildings of an Irish monastery were set within a rath – a circular enclosure with a fence around it. This fence was an important defence against attacks. It also helped to protect the monks from the temptation and sin of the world around them.

Inside the rath there were individual cells for the monks to live in and a number of larger shared buildings, like the refectory (dining hall).

Each monastery had a gatekeeper's lodge which had a guest room for travellers who needed to stay the night.

Some monasteries had schools attached to them. The rich people of the area sent their children to the monastic school as there was no other education system in Ireland at this time.

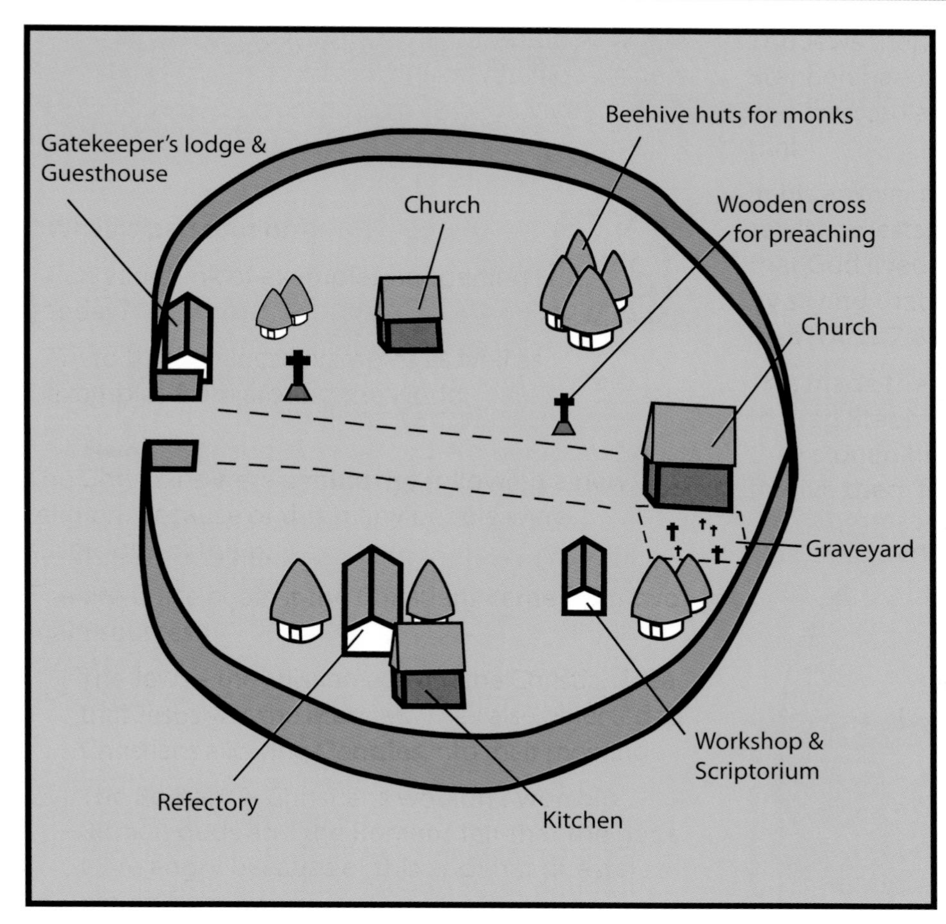


*A diagram of a typical monastery*

The church was always the central building in the monastery. Some monasteries also had a scriptorium or writing room. Here the monks would copy the scriptures by hand and **illuminate** them using beautiful decorative artwork.

The attention to detail given to this work shows how important the Bible was to the monks. They saw it as the word of God.

## *Food*

The food that the monks ate was very plain. Their everyday diet was bread and vegetables. **Fasting** was encouraged in many monasteries as a way of really concentrating on God.

As the monastery didn't have much contact with the outside world, much of what they ate was produced within the monastic enclosure. Therefore, farming was a very important part of the work carried out by the monks.

MI
BC

See what you can find out about the *Book of Kells*.

Where is it now?

Why is it important?

Find some examples of the artwork in the *Book of Kells*. Then write your name and illuminate it like the monks did.

## *Clothes*

The clothes worn by the monks were simple. They generally wore a long tunic with a hooded cloak over it, and sandals on their feet.

They often carried a staff (a long, strong stick) for protection when going on a journey outside the monastery.

## Daily life

A monk's daily life was made up of three activities:

1. Prayer
2. Study
3. Work – this could be either *physical* work like farming or *academic* work like teaching or working in the scriptorium.

The day was punctuated by services of worship. There could be up to seven set prayer times each day. Some monasteries expected the monks to get up during the night to say prayers as well.

Many monasteries were very strict. If a monk didn't obey the rules he would be punished. For example, a monk could be beaten or ordered into silence for not saying *"Amen"* when he should.

MI
TPD

Find out how monks live today.

Are there differences between the lives of monks today to their lives in the centuries just after Patrick?

Many monasteries also had large wooden or stone crosses. In Ireland, crosses had a special shape – they are called Celtic crosses. You can see a Celtic cross in the picture below on the left. The shapes in the Celtic cross are:

1. The cross – this is a symbol of Christ's death and resurrection.
2. The circle – this may represent eternity because it has no beginning and no end, or the halo around Christ's head which often appears in illustrations. It may also have symbolised the triumph of Christianity over paganism in Ireland, because of the circular laurel wreath worn by Roman commanders after winning a battle. Another idea is that the circle represented the sun. The Irish had been nature worshippers before the introduction of Christianity. Perhaps the circular shape was also a reminder of Jesus as the light of the world (John 8:2).
3. The Celtic knot – if unravelled, this consists of one or more circles. The unending lines stand for unending life or everlasting life available through Jesus Christ.

## Celtic cross

*A Celtic cross*

## Tower

*A reconstruction of a Celtic monastery at the Ulster History Park, County Tyrone*

Some monasteries had a round tower which had a door well above ground level. It was a safe place for the monks to hide themselves and their valuables during the Viking attacks.

These towers appeared later than the time of Patrick.

MI

1 What three activities made up most of the monks' day?

2 Why was the monastic fence so important?

3 Why did monasteries have to be self-sufficient?

4 What was the scriptorium used for?

5 What was the refectory used for?

Com
MI
BC
TPD

Imagine that you can travel back in time to AD 550 and live in a monastery.

Describe the living conditions, the clothes, the monastic enclosure and the way of life. Try to be creative.

# The Reformation

## Martin Luther (1483–1546)

MI
BC
TPD
Cit

What does 'reform' mean?

People can reform and things can reform.

Can you think of some recent examples?

Is reform always for the better?

In 1054 the Christian Church split into two parts – the Orthodox Church and the Catholic Church.

It split into many more parts in the sixteenth century during a period called the **Reformation**. This is a very important time in Christian Church history.

One of the most important people involved in the Reformation was a man called Martin Luther.

You are going to learn more about him, but first we will look at the times in which he lived.

MI

Which religious group do you think owes its name to Martin Luther?

## FACTORS WHICH LED TO THE REFORMATION

There were early efforts to make changes in the Church between 1300 and 1500.

In the Middle Ages people could not read the Bible for themselves because it was written in Latin. They depended on the priests to read it and teach them.

At Oxford University, a man named John Wycliffe stirred up controversy by translating the Bible into English. Jan Huss later translated Wycliffe's English Bible into Czech and was burned at the stake for doing so.

*The Jan Huss monument, Old Town Square, Prague. The statue was erected in 1915 to mark the five-hundredth anniversary of his death.*

In the sixteenth century the Catholic Church was a strong influence on most European countries. The **Pope** was a very powerful man. The leaders of the European countries had to pay large sums of money to Pope Leo X so that Saint Peter's **Basilica** in Rome could be built.

*Saint Peter's today*

Com MI TPD

Find out more about Saint Peter's in Rome.

How will you do this?

What are the questions you might ask about it?

Use your research to write a short history of the building.

What do you find most interesting about it?

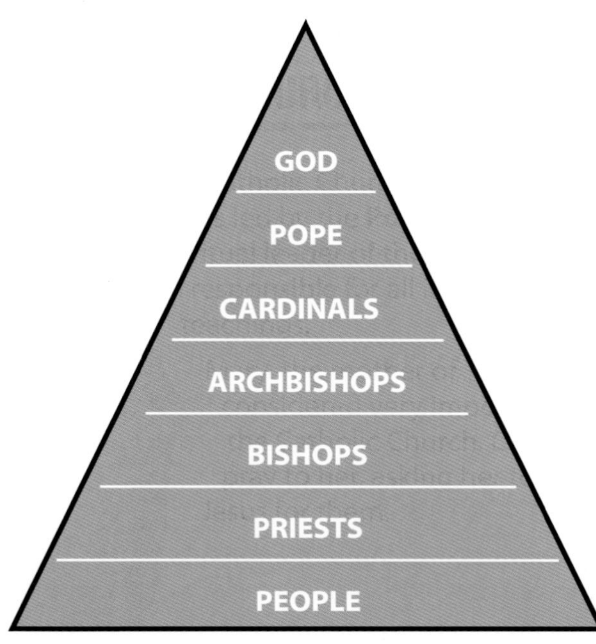

*The chain of command in the Catholic Church*

TPD PD

Is the Church the most important influence on people today, or are there other things which are more important?

Put the following in order of how important you think most people feel they are:

| Music | Magazines | Family |
|---|---|---|
| Bible | Minister | Friends |
| Celebrities | Television | Alcohol |

TPD

Put the following people into a chain with the most important person at the top: assistant teacher, principal, head of department, vice principal, and senior teacher.

MI TPD

1. When did the Reformation begin?
2. Why do you think many of the ordinary people living during the Middle Ages couldn't read or write?
3. Why might it be a bad thing not to be able to read or write? Think about things that you wouldn't be able to do, or that you would have to get other people to do for you.
4. Who was the most powerful man in the Church at this time?
5. Why were the people forced to pay taxes and how do you think they would have felt about it?

The Church also had an important influence on people's lives.

Daily life as well as Sunday worship was focused on the Church.

## *Erasmus (1466–1536)*

*A painting of Erasmus by Hans Holbein, 1523*

A scholar who attacked the Pope at this time was a Dutchman called Erasmus.

Although Erasmus was a Catholic, he criticised the Church and even turned down the chance to become a **cardinal** when it was offered to him.

The Church was teaching that the Pope could forgive sins. Erasmus didn't believe this.

Instead, he thought that faith in the death and resurrection of Jesus Christ, and not in the **sacraments** and **rituals** of the Church, was the only way to eternal life.

The most important thing that Erasmus did for the Reformation was to publish his Latin New Testament, which was based on the original Greek text.

Later, this was the book that Luther used to translate the Bible into German.

## *Exploring the unknown*

Until this time, Europeans thought they were at the centre of a small world made up of the three known continents (Europe, Africa and Asia) and the mysterious 'unknown'.

The explorations of people like Christopher Columbus began to change all this. The trade resulting from these explorations meant more wealth for many and led to the growth of cities.

## *The Renaissance*

**Renaissance** means 'rebirth' and refers to the rebirth of knowledge about the world, life and religion that took place during the fourteenth, fifteenth and sixteenth centuries, particularly in Italy, but also in Germany and other European countries.

This movement encouraged people to think again about old ideas, including the teaching of the Church.

The rethinking, questioning and criticism of the Church led to big changes, and it was Martin Luther who began the revolt that split the Church.

MI

Find out the names of famous writers, artists and musicians who were part of the Renaissance.

## LUTHER'S BACKGROUND

Martin Luther became unhappy about the Church and the behaviour of many priests. He believed that the leaders of the Church were out of touch with the needs of ordinary people, and many were rich and lived in luxury.

Martin Luther was born at Eisleben, Saxony, in modern Germany, on 10 November 1483. He was named after a saint, Martin of Tours.

He was the son of Hans and Margaret Luder, as the name was spelt then. Luther changed the spelling of his name when he was older.

Luther received his education at schools in Magdeburg and Eisenach. Later he studied at the University of Erfurt, where he earned a Bachelor's degree in 1501 and then a Master's degree.

His father had decided that Luther should become a lawyer. However, although things appeared to be going well for Luther, he was only staying on at the university to please his father. By now he had lost all interest in the law. Luther studied religion more and more and became worried about his sins.

## THE CALL TO BE A MONK

On 2 July 1505, Luther was returning to Erfurt after visiting his parents. He was suddenly caught in a violent thunderstorm. He was afraid and cried out to God to save him, promising that if he did so he would become a monk.

Luther kept his promise. When he returned to the university he sold his books, said goodbye to his friends, and entered the **Augustinian** monastery at Erfurt on 17 July 1505.

As a monk, Luther **fasted** and devoted many hours to prayer, **confession** and **pilgrimage**. In 1507 he became a priest. He continued to study and was awarded degrees which meant he was qualified to teach about the Bible. In 1512 he became Professor of Biblical Studies at the University of Wittenberg.

Luther became convinced that the Church had forgotten some of the key points of Christianity. For example, he felt that **salvation** could be gained only through believing in Christ alone, and not just by doing good deeds.

Com
MI
BC
TPD
WO

**The interview**

Split into groups. One person should take on the role of an interviewer.

Everybody else should take on the roles of important people in Luther's life, eg Luther himself, his father, and a friend from university.

The interviewer should then ask each person questions about Luther's life.

Here are some sample questions:

*To Luther:*

Where and when were you born?

Why did you decide to enter a monastery?

When did you become a priest?

*To Luther's father:*

Why did you send your son to university?

## INDULGENCES

In order to persuade people to give money for the building of Saint Peter's, Pope Leo X sold **indulgences**. An indulgence was a pardon from sin granted by the Church.

Priests travelled from Rome to sell indulgences and raise money. One was called John Tetzel and he came to Wittenberg in 1517 asking for donations in exchange for indulgences.

Luther objected to this. He felt that people would believe they could buy forgiveness for their wrongdoing. He decided to protest against the Church.

## LUTHER CHALLENGES THE CHURCH

**Some of the things Luther felt strongly about:**

That people could not 'buy off' their sins by paying money to the Church. Only God could forgive sins, not the Church.

That people were naturally sinful and should seek salvation by believing in God, making pilgrimages to holy places, and by doing good works

That priests should be subject to the law of the land in the same way as ordinary men and women

That priests were not **divine** beings

That all people should be allowed to read the Bible, not just priests. The Catholic Church believed that if all people were allowed to read the Bible they would form their own opinions and the Bible would become more important than the Church.

That the Church should not display rich images of saints and crucifixes, and that priests should not wear elaborate clothing

That priests did not have the power to turn the bread and wine into the body and blood of Christ during **Communion**

***Protest!***

Com
MI
WO
Cit

Can you think of organisations, groups or individuals today that protest?

What do they protest about?

Can you think of a protest that has happened recently in your area?

**Amnesty International**

Amnesty was started in 1961 by British lawyer Peter Benenson, after he read about two students being arrested in a cafe in Portugal for having a toast to freedom.

Amnesty now has over two million members and supporters around the world, including thousands in Northern Ireland.

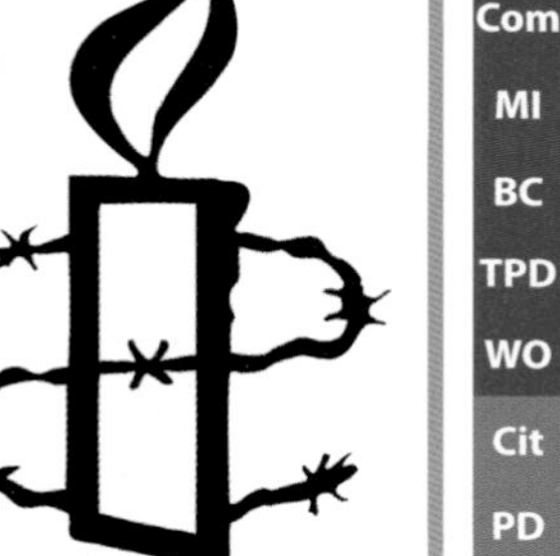

It is not a Christian organisation but Christians might support it because they agree that everyone is equally valuable.

Amnesty uses letter-writing, publicity campaigns and protests to make people aware of abuses of **human rights**.

Com ICT MI BC TPD Cit

Use the internet to research one of Amnesty's current protests.

You could use your findings to make a presentation to the rest of your class.

Com BC TPD WO Cit PD

**Hassle line**

Divide into two groups.

The groups should form two lines facing each other.

Your teacher will give each line a role like the example given below:

> Pupils in line 1 are *protesting against* an issue, eg a teenager protesting about having to be home by 11.00 pm.
>
> Pupils in line 2 are *defending* the issue, eg the father or mother saying why the teenager must be home by then.

Each pair of pupils facing each other should act out the situation.

At any point the teacher can shout out "Freeze!" and you should hold your pose.

If there's enough time your teacher might ask you to reverse your roles.

Afterwards, as a class discuss how you felt in your roles.

Com MI BC TPD WO Cit PD

**The Human Rights Act**

The Human Rights Act was adopted by the United Nations (UN) in 1948. The UN later set out the Convention on the Rights of the Child. The statements below are taken from this Convention.

Read them and think about them. Then discuss the questions below.

*Article 12:*
*The right to express opinions – the voice of the child should be listened to*
*(You have the right to give your opinion when decisions are being made that affect you.)*

*Article 15:*
*The right to freedom of association*
*(You have the right to meet and make friends with others.)*

*Article 16:*
*The right to privacy, honour and reputation*
*(You have the right to a private life, eg keeping a diary.)*

*Article 17:*
*The right to access information and media from national and international sources*
*(You have the right to collect information from books, the radio, television, etc.)*

If a child wants to do something but the adult in charge thinks the child shouldn't, what are the rights of the child?

What are the responsibilities of the adult?

A father reads his daughter's secret diary while she is out. He finds out that she has been taking drugs.
Think of the different ways he could react to this discovery.
What do *you* think her father should do?

## *Luther protests*

In October 1517, legend says that Luther pinned his '95 **Theses**' to the door of the Castle Church in Wittenberg and sent a copy to the **Archbishop**. The 95 Theses contained 95 points on indulgences. They were written in Latin – a language used only by scholars like Luther – so ordinary people would not have been able to read them.

*Luther pinning his 95 Theses to the church door*

There was nothing unusual about Luther nailing the Theses to the church door, as church doors were often used as noticeboards. You could put up an idea you had for others to read, and then prepare to discuss it.

But what happened after Luther nailed up his Theses *was* unusual. Someone made a copy, had it translated into German, and printed it so that the ordinary people could read what Luther had to say. Not everyone could read of course, but there were people who read it out in public places for others to hear. Luther's views spread very quickly.

**Some of Luther's 95 Theses**

5 The Pope doesn't have the power to let people off from their sins.

21 People are wrong to think that by paying for indulgences they will not be punished by God for their sins.

86 The Pope is very rich. Why doesn't he build Saint Peter's using his own money instead of taking it from poor people?

Luther's 95 Theses were supposed to be a list of things that he wanted to discuss with other churchmen. However, his ideas were supported by many people and so he started to criticise other practices in the Catholic Church, such as having statues in church buildings.

The invention of the printing press in the previous century helped spread Luther's ideas to other parts of Europe.

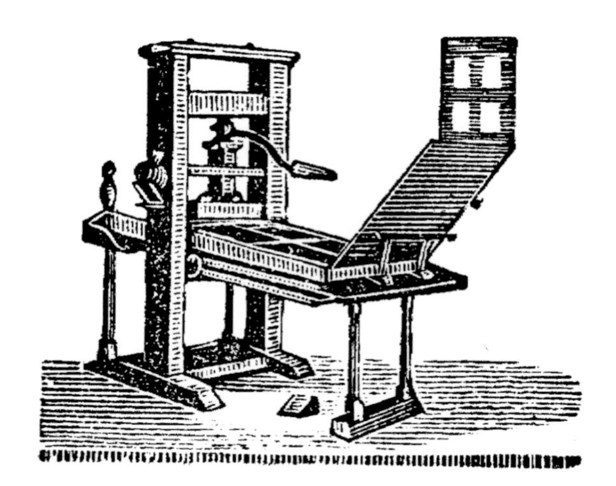

*An early printing press*

Com BC TPD WO Cit

What do people do today when they disagree with something?

What modern forms of protest are there?

Split into groups and choose an issue that is important to all of you. It could be to do with your local area, or it could be an international issue.

Decide how you would make people aware of this issue and join your protest.

Com BC TPD WO

In groups, create your own theses.

Instead of 95 you are being challenged to produce ten theses to take to the school council. Your topic is things you would like to change about school.

How would you present your list of ten theses to the school council?

What forms of presentation could you use?

Your task as a group is to present your ten theses to your class as if it was the school council.

MI TPD

Where do you think the name 'Protestant' comes from?

What would not paying for indulgences mean for the people?

Luther was not the first to criticise the Church, but his protest was the beginning of change.

## THE BEGINNING OF PROTESTANTISM

MI

Fill in the blanks with the words from the box below:

The nailing of the ________ Theses to the door of the church was the beginning of the Reformation. Many people agreed with Luther's ideas and gave him support. This group ________ against the Catholic Church and became known as ________.

Therefore, the Protestant religion dates back to ________.

Although many people supported Luther, they were afraid to speak out against the Church. Anyone discovered condemning the Church was accused of being a ________ and was severely punished.

| | |
|---|---|
| *Protestants* | *95* |
| *heretic* | *protested* |
| *1517* | |

### *Heretics*

TPD Cit

Look at the headlines below. Why might these people have suffered **intolerance**?

MAN BADLY BEATEN IN FIVEMILETOWN

NEW FAMILY IN LISNASKEA FORCED TO LEAVE THEIR HOME IN EARLY HOURS OF THE MORNING

Now look at the picture below.

What does it show?

How does it make you feel?

Do you think people should be allowed to write words like these on walls?

TPD Cit

In Northern Ireland, people are sometimes intolerant of symbols. Can you think of any examples?

ICT MI TPD Cit

Use newspapers, magazines and the internet to find three recent examples of intolerance of any sort which happened *outside* Northern Ireland.

Com
TPD
SM
Cit

**Spectrum debate**

*"Northern Ireland is the most intolerant country in Europe."*

Imagine there is a line down the centre of your classroom. One end represents complete agreement with the statement above, and the other end represents complete disagreement.

Think about your opinion on the statement and then take a position along the line.

Your teacher will ask you why you've chosen that position. After listening to what your classmates have to say, you can change your position on the line, but be ready to explain why!

Com
MI
TPD
WO
Cit

Look at the picture above.

What is going on in this picture?

How does it make you feel?

What does it make you wonder?

Find out other ways heretics were punished at the time.

Could anything like this happen today?

**Heretics** faced very slow and public executions. They were given such terrible punishments because speaking out against the Catholic Church was considered one of the worst crimes a person could commit.

They were often burned in public to set an example to other people. Anyone who was thinking about speaking out against the Church might have changed their mind whenever they saw what could happen to them.

## EXCOMMUNICATION

News of Luther's protest spread quickly. He was supported and helped by some powerful German princes who didn't like the power the Pope had over them.

Copies of books which Luther wrote were burned by the Catholic Church. The Church tried to persuade him to take back what he had said, but Luther refused and he was sent an order throwing him out of the Church. This is called **excommunication**. Luther showed that he was not worried about this by burning it on a bonfire in Wittenberg.

Luther didn't want to leave the Church he had grown up in. He simply wanted to see it changed for the better – in other words, *reformed*.

*Luther burning the order of excommunication*

Com
TPD
WO

Look at the picture at the bottom right of the opposite page.

What does this picture tell us about what Luther thought of his punishment?

How do we know he had support?

Do you think this picture shows how it really would have been?

## THE DIET OF WORMS

Charles V (the **Holy Roman Emperor**) and many other churchmen believed that Luther's ideas were dangerous.

They also realised that if many people followed these ideas the Church would lose much of its power, so something had to be done to stop him.

In 1521, Charles V ordered Luther to appear before the Imperial **Diet** in Worms, a city near Mainz in modern Germany. The Imperial Diet was a meeting of rulers in the **Holy Roman Empire**.

The members of the Diet insisted that only the Pope had the authority to say what the Bible meant – not Luther or anyone else. They didn't agree with Luther's idea of reformation.

When Luther refused to take back anything he had said, Charles V issued the Edict of Worms on 25 May 1521. This meant:

Luther was an outlaw.

His writings were banned.

There was a warrant for his arrest.

So as a result of the Edict of Worms Luther was no longer safe. On his way back from Worms he was taken to Wartburg Castle by the Duke of Saxony's men, to live in safety until things calmed down.

Luther lived at the castle for a year, translating the Bible from Latin into German.

The New Testament was printed in 1522 and is thought to have sold 5,000 copies in two months.

Along with the help of others, the whole Bible was translated into German and published in 1534.

## A NEW CHURCH

Luther eventually came out of hiding. The Edict of Worms was never enforced, so he was safe from punishment.

Many others broke away from the Catholic Church and these people later became known as **Protestants**.

One branch of Protestantism was the Church Luther started himself, which was called **Lutheran**.

Luther's final break with the Catholic Church came in 1525 when he married Katharina von Bora, who had been a nun. They lived in a former Augustinian monastery in Wittenberg.

They were very happily married and Luther declared:

Luther died in 1546 and was buried in the Castle Church in Wittenberg, near the pulpit.

*The Castle Church today*

MI
TPD

1 Why were the Pope and other churchmen concerned about Luther's ideas?
2 Who helped Luther at Worms?
3 What was the name of Luther's Church and what did his followers later become known as?
4 What happened in 1525?
5 Why is Luther's marriage so important in telling us what he thought about the Catholic Church?
6 Why do you think Luther was buried near the pulpit?

Ma

Crack the code to reveal information about Luther's new Church.

**a=1 b=2 c=3 and so on**

Luther's new Church was quite different from the Catholic Church. The services were 19 9 13 16 12 5 18 and were in German, not 12 1 20 9 14. They were mainly made up of Bible readings, 19 5 18 13 15 14 19 and hymn singing.

The new Church was governed by a council of 2 9 19 8 15 16 19 and not by the Pope. The new Church 16 18 15 20 5 19 20 5 4 against 3 1 20 8 15 12 9 3 beliefs, so it was called the Protestant Church. Many kings and princes accepted Protestantism because they no longer had to pay 20 1 24 5 19 to the Catholic Church or obey the 16 15 16 5. This gave the 11 9 14 7 19 more power in their own countries.

Luther's ideas soon spread to Norway, 19 23 5 4 5 14, Denmark, 9 3 5 12 1 14 4, the Netherlands, northern Germany, England and 19 3 15 20 12 1 14 4.

In Geneva a French man called 10 15 8 14 3 1 12 22 9 4 formed a Protestant Church, and Calvinistic Churches were started in France and the Netherlands. In France, Protestants became known as 8 21 7 21 5 14 15 20 19. In 1534 the Church of England was set up by 8 5 14 18 25 VIII who made himself head of the Church.

Later, many **Nonconformist** organisations were formed, including the 13 5 20 8 15 4 9 19 20 19. This Church was founded by John and Charles 23 5 19 12 5 25, who were **converted** in 1738.

**Martin Luther fact file**

The Church leaders in Rome called Luther *"the Beast"*.

In England, King Henry VIII wrote a tract saying how wrong Luther was. The Pope then gave Henry the special title 'Defender of the Faith'.

King Henry's daughter, Mary Tudor, called Luther a "***fanatic***".

People who left Europe to live in America took Luther's teaching with them.

Other Protestants, such as John Calvin, also spread the movement for reform.

MI

Now make your own Martin Luther fact file by listing five things you have found out about him from reading this book.

**Key dates in the Reformation**

| | |
|---|---|
| 1300s | John Wycliffe led an early movement for the reform of the Catholic Church. |
| 1517 | On 31 October Martin Luther posted his 95 Theses at Wittenberg. The Reformation had begun. |
| 1519 | In Switzerland, a reformer named Ulrich Zwingli began a campaign against the sale of indulgences within the Church. |
| 1521 | Luther was excommunicated from the Catholic Church. |
| 1526 | The First Diet of Speyer (a city in Germany) met and decided that German princes could follow Lutheran teachings. |
| 1529 | The Second Diet of Speyer overturned the ruling of the first. Lutheran princes issued a protest against it, and therefore became known as the Protestants. |
| 1534 | Protestantism was established in England. Henry VIII had been arguing with the Pope for years because he wanted to divorce his wife, Catherine of Aragon. The Pope excommunicated him and Henry set up the Church of England. |
| 1545 | The Council of Trent met. This marked the beginning of the Catholic Reformation, when reforms were introduced to try to stop people becoming Protestants. |
| 1549 | Edward VI issued the Book of Common Prayer, which is a book for using in worship in the **Anglican** Church. |

Com ICT MI BC TPD

Imagine you are a national newspaper reporter. You are covering the Reformation and you must write an article for your newspaper.

How will you report the events surrounding the 95 Theses and the beginning of the Reformation?

Remember to include the following:

- A title for the newspaper, eg *Berlin Star*
- Answers to who, what, where, why, and when
- A headline for the article
- Interviews highlighting important people, eg Tetzel and Luther
- Pictures to accompany your article, eg Luther

You could use a computer to design your article.

Com MI BC TPD

Choose an issue to do with the Reformation and take a position on it, eg the 95 Theses, or indulgences.

You could take on the role of a priest or a supporter of Luther.

Write a letter to the editor of a newspaper describing how you feel about the issue you have chosen.

Use persuasive language to convince the newspaper's readers of your point of view.

# THE COUNTER-REFORMATION

TPD
PD

Imagine the following things happen. For each of them, what would you do next?

Your mobile phone rings in class.

You didn't revise for your summer exams and you've just realised they start tomorrow.

Your alarm doesn't go off and you were supposed to meet up with a friend half an hour ago.

Every *action* has a *reaction*. This was the case with the Catholic Church. When it was being criticised, it reacted.

The Counter-Reformation was an organised response to Protestant criticisms. Even before Luther posted his 95 Theses in 1517, change was taking place in the Catholic Church.

TPD

What sort of problems might the Church have been facing as a result of the Reformation?

TPD
Cit

How might people in charge react to a protest, eg in your school or the place where you live?

What might they do?

## *The Council of Trent*

Martin Luther didn't think the Pope should have the final say on what happened to him. Instead, he thought a general council of the Church should make the decision and so he appealed to them.

For centuries popes had claimed that they had supreme authority in the Church. This had been handed down from Jesus to the **apostle** Peter, and then passed down from pope to pope. This was accepted in Rome but many people outside Rome disagreed with it.

The Council of Trent is one of the most important events in the Counter-Reformation.

Ma

Work out the calculation to discover when the Council of Trent first met:

$((9 \times 51) + 56) \times (5 - 2)$

Work out the calculation to discover when the Council of Trent ended:

$((70 \times 91) - 118) \div (9 - 5)$

The Council of Trent was set up by Pope Paul III. The point of the Council was to work out the problems in the Catholic Church, and to decide once and for all where it stood on all the issues Luther and other Protestants disagreed with.

1. The Council made it absolutely clear what Catholics should believe about salvation, the sacraments and even what books should be in the Bible.
2. It stopped the sale of indulgences and made rules for the priests to follow to prevent corruption.
3. It also said that the Pope was the head of the Church and that he was the only one with the right to interpret the Bible.
4. The Council also asked for a new **catechism** to be produced. This was called the Roman Catechism.

The Council of Trent is a very important part of the history of the Catholic Church.

Com
MI
TPD
WO

Find out where Trent is, and where the Council of Trent met.

Now look up Matthew 16:19. Discuss what *you* think Jesus meant by what he said to Peter.

### *The Index*

To make sure no Catholic read anything that might lead them astray, Pope Paul IV published the **Index** in 1557.

The Index was a list of books that no Catholic was supposed to read.

All of Martin Luther's works were included on the list, as well as some translations of the Bible.

### *Reforming Orders*

Of course, many Catholics had believed for a long time that it was important to change the Church from the inside. Often, these reformers began their own groups to improve the things that they felt were wrong.

One early example of a reforming **Order** was the **Franciscan Order**. It was founded by Saint Francis of Assisi, who was born in Italy and lived from 1182–1226.

Franciscans were known for observing priestly duties strictly. They lived life in complete poverty and didn't own anything.

There are still groups of Franciscans today, including the 'Poor Clares' who are nuns.

Many of the stories about Saint Francis tell of his love for animals, and according to legend he once gave a sermon to a flock of birds. He is the patron saint of animals.

Saint Francis is specially remembered every year on 4 October. Around this time, many churches hold services where animals are blessed.

The most powerful and important of the reforming Orders was the **Society of Jesus**.

It was founded in 1534 by Ignatius of Loyola, who ran the society like an army and demanded complete obedience.

Its priests were known as the **Jesuits**. The Jesuits took a special interest in missionary work, education, and helping the poor and sick.

They were intelligent, **zealous** men and were very successful in slowing the spread of Protestantism.

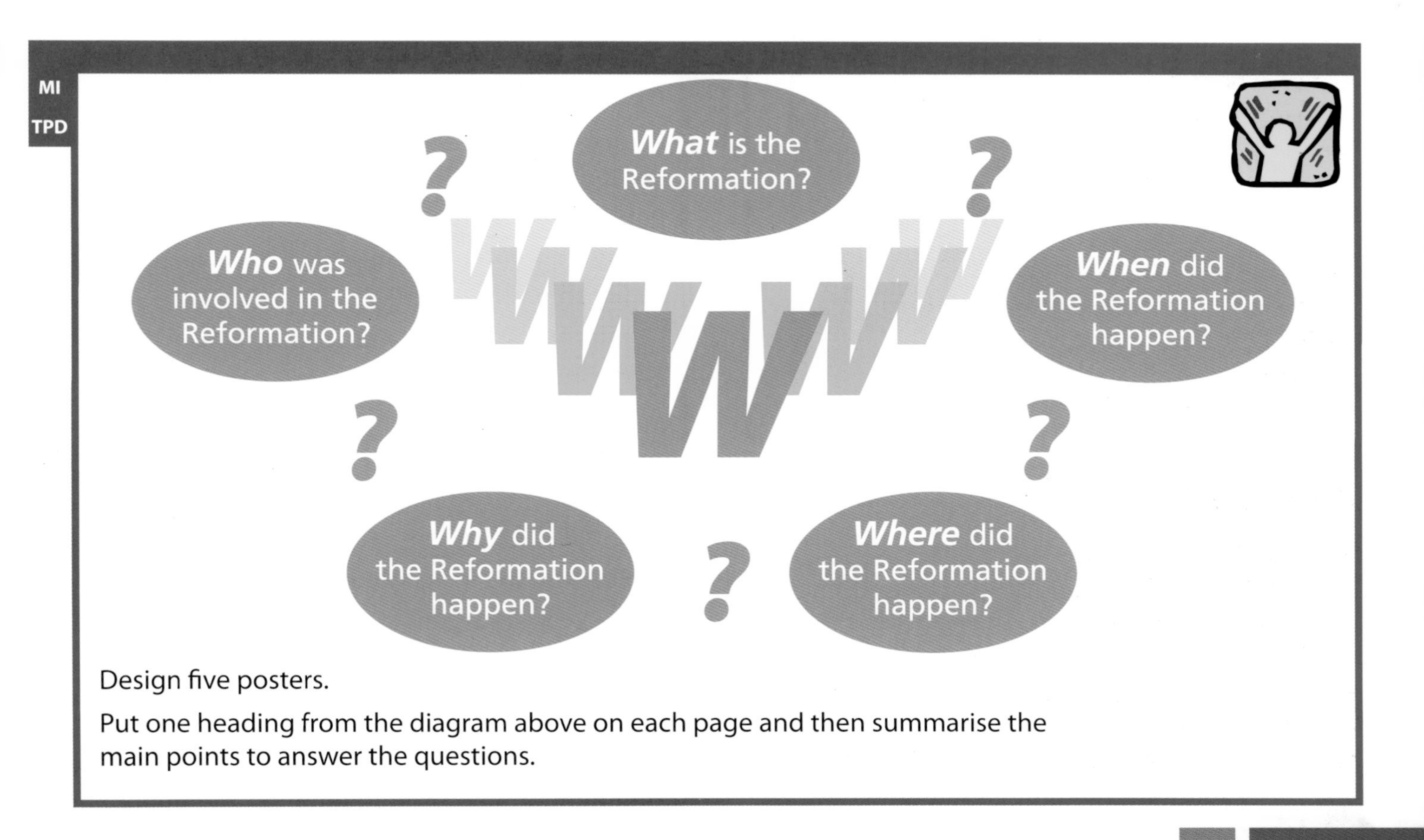


Design five posters.

Put one heading from the diagram above on each page and then summarise the main points to answer the questions.

# Eighteenth and nineteenth-century Christian outreach and social reformers

## William Wilberforce (1759–1833)

EfE Cit PD

What would you like to be remembered for?
Climbing Everest?
Being a famous pop star?
Scoring a goal for Northern Ireland?
Inventing a new product?
Winning the Belfast Marathon?

*Laurence Griffiths/Getty Images Sport/Getty Images*

*David Healy after scoring a hat trick in Northern Ireland's Euro 2008 qualifying match against Spain, 6 September 2006, Windsor Park, Belfast*

Today, over 170 years after his death, we remember William Wilberforce for being the leader of the campaign to end **slavery** and the **slave trade**.

He was a man who used his life to make a difference.

*A portrait of William Wilberforce*

MI TPD

**Order! Order!**

Below are some statements about the life and work of William Wilberforce.

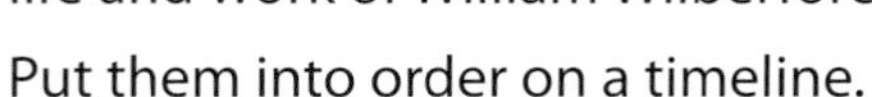

Put them into order on a timeline.

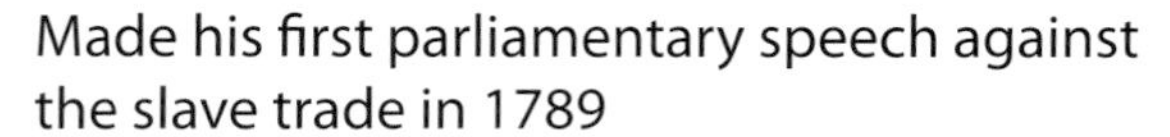

- Made his first parliamentary speech against the slave trade in 1789
- Died in 1833 and buried in Westminster Abbey
- Got married in 1797
- Retired from politics in 1825
- Elected a Member of Parliament (MP) in 1780 at the age of 21
- Born in 1759 in Hull in the north of England
- Became a Christian in 1784
- Studied at Saint John's College, Cambridge, in 1776
- Trading of slaves made illegal in the British Empire in 1807

## WILBERFORCE'S BACKGROUND

William Wilberforce was born in Hull, a seaport in the north of England, in 1759. He was the son of a rich merchant.

After the death of his father, his mother became very ill so Wilberforce was sent to live with an aunt and uncle. They had a strong Christian faith and took him to the local Methodist church.

When he was 17 he went to Saint John's College, Cambridge. One of his closest friends at Saint John's was William Pitt, who became Britain's youngest Prime Minister at the age of 24 in 1783.

Many of Wilberforce's friends, including Pitt, were the sons of important politicians. Wilberforce had no interest in anything to do with religion at Cambridge and preferred to party with his friends.

TPD

Find out what happened when Wilberforce left university by rearranging the boxes below.

| university he | ecome a poli | decided to b |
|---|---|---|
| tician and h | ted to represent H | When Wilberf |
| orce left | ull at the age of 21. | e was elec |

Wilberforce's new profession was not going to make him rich but he didn't need money because he came from a wealthy family.

He was not yet a Christian when he was elected.

Com
MI
BC
TPD

Wilberforce had to persuade the people of Hull to vote for him. Politicians in the eighteenth century often bribed people to get votes. Once, William held a feast to get people to vote for him. However, not everyone liked politicians – he found this out when he had a stone thrown at him!

Coming up to elections politicians in Northern Ireland also visit villages and towns to **canvass** voters. They send leaflets in the post and put up posters.

Your challenge is to design an election poster. Include the following:

- Party name, eg the Teenage Party
- Information about you, eg I am confident
- Promises if people vote for you, eg a skateboarding park
- Your picture

## CHRISTIANITY CALLS

In 1784 Wilberforce went on a tour of Europe. While he was touring, he read about Christianity and talked about it with other travellers.

Reverend John Newton was also a friend and influenced him very much. Newton wrote the famous hymn 'Amazing Grace'. He used to be the captain of a slave ship, but his life changed when he became a Christian after surviving a terrible storm at sea. He was the minister of the church Wilberforce went to as a child.

Wilberforce decided to become a Christian. He wasn't sure if he could serve both God and his country because many politicians bribed, lied and gambled.

However, Wilberforce's friends convinced him that he could still be a politician, but he would be a different type of one. Everyone who met him was amazed by the change in his life.

As a Christian MP, Wilberforce supported many good causes. His main interest was fighting to end slavery because he believed it was wrong for people to own other people.

He knew that this might cost him friends but felt he had to stand up for what he believed in.

# SLAVERY

Com BC TPD WO Cit PD

Wilberforce's aim in life became the ending of slavery.

What is your aim or aims? Talk about your ideas with the rest of the class.

Then as a class make a collage to reflect some of these aims.

## *What is slavery?*

A slave is a person who is owned by someone else. They have no choice, no freedom and no money. Slaves have to do the work their master tells them to. They may be punished for not following orders.

Slavery has existed for a long time. For example, slaves were used by the Romans.

*The deck of a slave ship*

Com TPD WO Cit

Look at the picture above.

How do you think it would have felt to be one of these people on their way to be sold as slaves?

## *Slavery in Britain*

About 15 million slaves were taken from West Africa between 1540 and 1850. Britain became the world leader in the slave trade. British ships sailed to West Africa and brought black people to serve as slaves in England and North America.

The more slaves a ship could carry, the more money could be made. Slaves were chained up and had little room to move. They often arrived suffering from lack of food, sea sickness and disease.

Many died during their journey at sea from diseases like smallpox. Others were crippled for life because of the way they had been chained up. The cruelty of the white masters and the terrible smells made life on board very hard.

To hide the ill health of the slaves from possible buyers, they were fattened up and coated in oil before being sold at market. The dull skin of a slave was seen as a sign of ill health.

TPD

Guess if these sentences are true or false.

1 Many slaves were marked with branding irons.
2 The death rate on the slave ships was 50%.
3 Slaves were worked so hard that few lived longer than 20 years after they became slaves.
4 Royal Navy sailors said that they could smell slave ships two miles away.
5 As many as 500 slaves could be packed on a ship into a 30-metre long space below deck.

*Answers: 1 True. 2 True. 3 False – 9 years. 4 False – 10 miles. 5 False – 200.*

Slave traders argued that they were giving their slaves a better life because they had been facing execution after being captured in African wars.

Wilberforce sent people to investigate the conditions on slave ships. He used what he learnt to fight slavery.

In May 1789 Wilberforce made his first speech in Parliament against the slave trade. As a result, he was seen as one of the leaders of the anti-slave movement. His speech lasted three hours!

In 2007, a film was made about Wilberforce. It was called *Amazing Grace*. The part of Wilberforce was played by the actor Ioan Gruffudd.

On one occasion, Wilberforce said:

*The [Slave] Trade, founded in inequity and carried on as this was [must be* ***abolished****]. Let the policy be what it might, let the consequences be what they would, I am from this time determined that I [will] never rest until I have effected its abolition.*

For the next 18 years Wilberforce brought up the subject of slavery in Parliament again and again, but didn't get very far.

At first his work seemed to be a waste of time but then something happened. On 25 March 1807 Parliament finally made the *slave trade* illegal in the British Empire.

Wilberforce felt that *slavery* itself should have been banned because those who were already slaves could still be kept and used.

He continued to speak against slavery both in Parliament and in public meetings until he resigned from Parliament in 1825.

## *The Slavery Abolition Act*

It was not until 1833 that slavery itself was ended in the British Empire by the Slavery Abolition Act.

Slaves were to be given their freedom within a year of the Act. Their masters were given **compensation**. About 800,000 slaves were set free.

Slavery and the slave trade had been abolished in the British Empire, but it was to be another 32 years before slavery was also ended in America.

1807 – Abolition of the slave trade in the British Empire. One million people living in slavery.

1808 – Abolition of the slave trade in the United States (US)

1833 – Abolition of slavery in the British Empire

1865 – Abolition of slavery in the US

*Abolition of slave trade timeline*

## *Wilberforce's death*

Wilberforce died three days after the Slavery Abolition Act was passed. He had achieved his goal. He is buried in Westminster Abbey. It is a very great honour to be buried there.

… His name will ever be specially identified with those exertions

Which, by the blessing of God, removed from England

The guilt of the African Slave Trade,

and prepared the way for the Abolition of Slavery in every colony of the Empire …

*From a plaque to Wilberforce in Westminster Abbey*

*Westminster Abbey today*

MI
TPD

Many famous people are buried in Westminster Abbey. At first only kings and queens were buried there, but now the church contains the graves of many other well-known people.

Look at this list:

- David Livingstone
- Sir Winston Churchill
- Sir Isaac Newton
- Geoffrey Chaucer
- Oliver Cromwell

What are these people known for? See if you can find out.

# POLITICS AND GOVERNMENT

TPD
Cit

How much do you know about the government and Parliament?

Match the words to the right definition.

| | |
|---|---|
| **Speaker** | When everybody can vote for those they want to represent them |
| **MP (Member of Parliament)** | The person who leads the government of the United Kingdom (UK) |
| **The opposition** | A person elected to the UK Parliament |
| **Election** | A person elected to the Northern Ireland Assembly |
| **MLA (Member of the Legislative Assembly)** | The person who leads the government of Northern Ireland |
| **First Minister** | An area which elects MPs or MLAs |
| **Constituency** | The political party which is against the government |
| **Prime Minister** | The chairperson of debates in Parliament or the Assembly |

Can you think of any other words that are to do with Parliament or the government?

What do they mean?

### *Governing Northern Ireland*

*Parliament Buildings at Stormont, Belfast, where the Northern Ireland Assembly meets*

# Northern Ireland Assembly

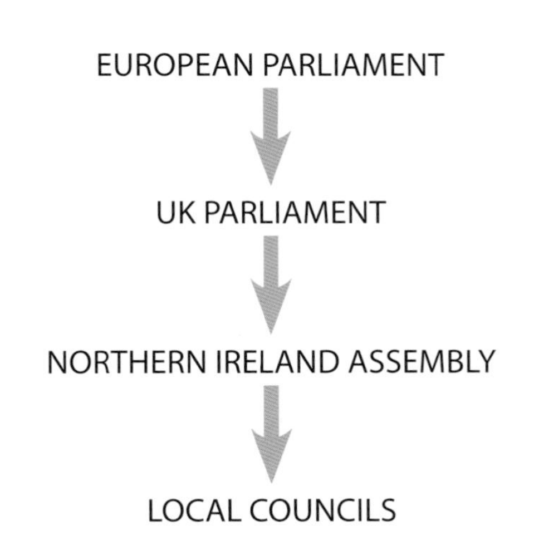


*The structure of government*

Com
MI
BC
TPD
Cit

Find out the number of MLAs in Northern Ireland, their names and the political parties they represent.

Then see what you can find out about the typical day of an MLA.
You could email or write to an MLA. Most MLAs have their own websites. You could also try searching the website of the Northern Ireland Assembly.

Finally, choose an MLA and produce a mini-biography for them.

## *A day in the life of an MLA*

### Iris Robinson

Iris Robinson is a member of the Democratic Unionist Party (DUP). She is an MLA and the MP for Strangford.

Iris has to split her time between her constituency, the Assembly and the Houses of Parliament in London.

You can read about a typical day for Iris below.

**6.55 am:**
Fly from Heathrow to George Best Belfast City Airport

**8.10 am:**
Arrive in Belfast; travel home for change of clothing and freshen up

**9.00 am:**
Travel to constituency office in Newtownards; get update from office manager; sign off letters to constituents and public bodies, etc; read new correspondence

**10.30 am:**
Surgery in Portavogie. One Friday of each month I hold a surgery in different parts of my constituency. This is because some people, like elderly or sick people, can't travel into Ards but still want to meet me face to face. At the surgery I try to help my constituents with their problems.

**12.00 pm:**
Home visits, for constituents who aren't able to leave the house

**1.00 pm:**
Back at Ards office. The office is closed over lunch so I use the quiet to record on my Dictaphone some letters I need sent out from this morning's surgery and home visits. I also list things I need my staff to do while I'm at Parliament to start sorting out the problems people have brought me.

**2.30 pm:**
Hold appointments at Ards office. They are meant to last 15 minutes each and I try to fit four in every afternoon. Mostly they end up running over 15 minutes but my staff take this into account when they arrange the diary.

**4.00 pm:**
Site meeting in Ballygowan with Roads Service/Planning Service about a case I am dealing with

**4.30 pm:**
Meeting with Housing Executive District Manager about another case I am dealing with

**5.00 pm:**
Head back to Dundonald for another site meeting, about disabled parking outside a house

**6.00 pm:**
Arrive home; change and get ready for hosting event for health group at Stormont. I am speaking at the event so I need to check my speech.

**7.30 pm:**
Event at Stormont. I make a speech on health matters and meet and greet local representatives.

**10.30 pm:**
Return home and prepare for events I've agreed to attend over the weekend

## Alasdair McDonnell

Alasdair McDonnell is a member of the Social Democratic and Labour Party (SDLP). He is an MLA and the MP for South Belfast.

Alasdair has to split his time between his constituency, the Assembly and the Houses of Parliament in London.

You can read about a typical day for Alasdair below.

**9.00–9.15 am:**
Walk children to school. I'm always very busy so this is one of my most enjoyable parts of the day. I'm often home late in the evenings when the children are in bed, so I try as much as possible to be the one who gets them ready in the mornings.

**10.00–11.30 am:**
Dealing with correspondence. This is when I respond to my constituents' and other organisations' concerns about a wide range of problems and issues. My staff can often handle enquiries but I need to personally sort out difficult cases. Often a letter from an MP can do the trick.

**11.30 am–12.15 pm:**
Meeting with District Police Commander and local constituents. Sometimes constituents have difficulty sorting out problems and need me to set up meetings with police, planners or other branches of government. This meeting involved a family that had suffered from intimidation and anti-social behaviour where they live, and wanted the police to take action.

**12.20–1.00 pm:**
Interview at the BBC. I am often asked to give media interviews, many on the peace process in Northern Ireland. This is an important part of being a politician as it lets people know what their representatives are doing for them and raises public awareness of many issues. This helps my constituents and my party.

**1.15–2.15 pm:**
Attending launch of an advice centre in my constituency. One way of getting the support and help of an MP is to invite them to different events.

**2.30–3.30 pm:**
Preparation for London at office. I deal with more enquiries from my constituents and prepare for my attendance at Parliament. My staff help me find out what will be happening at Parliament while I'm there, eg what votes are taking place and which debates I can take part in.

**3.45–4.15 pm:**
I drive back to my house and pick up an overnight bag and the papers I'll need for my time over at Parliament. Then it's straight to the airport.

**5.40–7.05 pm:**
Fly to London

**8.30–9.30 pm:**
Attend a parliamentary briefing with other MPs. Events can happen at Parliament until late in the evening. But this suits me as I like to pack as much into my time there as possible.

Com
MI
BC
TPD
WO
Cit

Choose one of the activities below.

**Take action!**

Write a letter to an MP on an issue you feel strongly about. Ask them to take action.

Here are some ideas of what you could ask about:

- Pollution
- The litter problem
- Poverty
- **Discrimination** and **prejudice**
- Roads
- Hospitals
- The lack of facilities for young people in your area

**The interview**

Your local radio station is interviewing an MP on something the MP feels strongly about. The interviewer does not agree with the MP's views.

Work in pairs and decide which role each of you will take. Think about what you're going to say, then perform a role play of the interview.

**The debate**

The whole class can be involved in this activity – the more people the better!

In a debate there are some special roles. You will need to appoint a speaker, two clerks, a proposer and an opposer.

How does the debate work?

- The speaker will ask the first clerk to read the motion (the issue being debated).
- The proposer represents those in favour of the motion. They will speak first, followed by people supporting the motion.
- The opposer represents those against the motion. They will now speak, followed by those supporting what they say.
- The speaker will then tell people to start voting.
- The second clerk will count the votes and announce the result of the debate.

Suggestion for a debate: *"This house believes that homework should be banned."*

## SLAVERY TODAY

Slavery hasn't disappeared. It still exists in the twenty-first century.

It has returned because of changes in the economy and society. Things like corruption, and populations getting bigger in countries in the developing world, have been part of this.

Some people think that almost one million people are traded every year. Many of them are women and children.

Often people in poorer countries are forced into near-slavery, working in poor conditions in **sweatshops**.

Many **multinationals** use these sweatshops to produce goods such as MP3 players or copies of designer clothing. This is because they can pay people very little.

Then these goods are imported into countries like Britain and Ireland where they are sold very cheap.

This is what United Nations (UN) Secretary-General Kofi Annan said about slavery in December 2004:

*Let us reaffirm our commitment to **abolish** slavery from every country, and ensure that the rights and dignity of people everywhere are respected.*

# William Booth (1829–1912)

Time & Life Pictures/Stringer/Getty Images

*William Booth in 1900*

William Booth was born in 1829 in Nottingham, England. At first his family were quite well off, but his father made some bad decisions about money, and soon they began having money problems. William had to drop out of school as his parents could not pay the fees any more.

To help support his family, Booth became an apprentice in a pawnbroker's. He didn't like his job but it made him see the poverty around him and people's suffering.

Com TPD WO

What is a pawnbroker?

Why might people go to one?

Why do you think William Booth did not like his job?

When he was a teenager, Booth became a Christian. Later in life he married Catherine Mumford.

He became a Methodist minister, and spoke of *"darkest England"* because people knew so little about God or Christianity.

Booth was constantly in demand as a speaker but he felt that God wanted more than just preaching from him. He wanted to do more to reach the ordinary people who were in so much need.

In 1865 Booth and his wife set up the Christian Mission. Booth and his followers preached but also practised what they believed through active social work.

They opened 'Food for the Million' shops or soup kitchens, which gave out food to hungry people. In 1878 the name of the organisation was changed to the **Salvation** Army.

TPD

On one occasion William Booth said:

*"While women weep, as they do now, I'll fight; while little children go hungry, as they do now, I'll fight; while men go to prison, in and out, in and out, as they do now, I'll fight; while there is a drunkard left, while there is a poor lost girl upon the streets, while there remains one dark soul without the light of God, I'll fight – I'll fight to the very end."*

Think about the name he gave his organisation. Is it a good one?

TPD

Philip Gibbs, a journalist for the *Daily Mail*, met William Booth in 1902. This is what he said about him:

*"His spirit was like a white flame. He had a burning fire within him."*

If you met someone who had been described like that, what do you think they would be like?

The Salvation Army is still going strong today. Its members wear a uniform, they are called soldiers and they belong to a **corps**. The Salvation Army is a Christian Church and a charity, and helps the poor and underprivileged, such as the homeless, alcoholics and drug addicts.

One of the ways it raises money is by selling its magazine, *The War Cry*. Its members also give money regularly, people can make donations, and there are yearly appeals to raise money.

Com TPD WO Cit

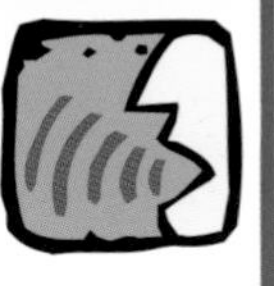

If you could meet Booth now, what would you still want to know about him? What questions would you ask him?

The pictures on this page show some of the work that the Salvation Army does in Northern Ireland and the Republic of Ireland today.

*Above: An organised outing. Many of the corps have minibuses and organise outings for older members, or even collect them and bring them to the corps on Sunday or for activities during the week.*

*Above and left: The Care and Share Shop on the Newtownards Road, Belfast.*
*The shop provides quality clothing and bric-a-brac at low prices.*
*The building also has a drop-in coffee shop, where people can call and have a chat or just a cup of tea or coffee.*
*Profits from Salvation Army charity shops help fund further community work.*

*Above: A chaplain talking to one of the people staying at a Salvation Army residential home in Holywood*

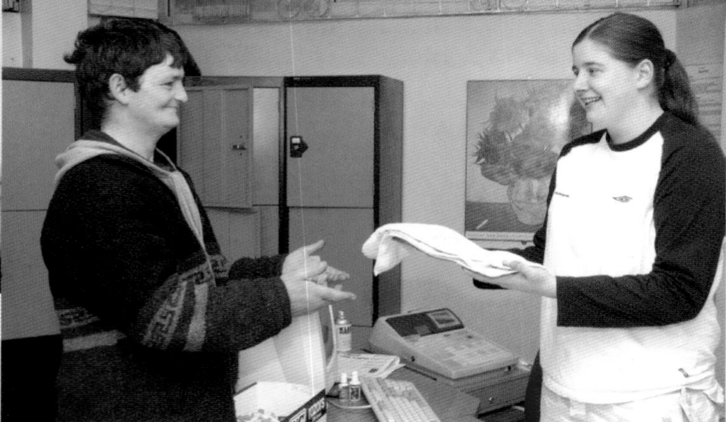

*Above: A worker providing a towel for a homeless person who has come into a Salvation Army centre in Dublin to have a shower*

# AN INTERVIEW WITH A MEMBER OF THE SALVATION ARMY

**Name: Neil McFerran**

**Age: 37**

**Rank: Captain**

Captains Susan and Neil McFerran

*When did you become a member of the Salvation Army and what made you want to join?*

*I became a member in 1986.*

*I came to the Salvation Army youth activities and the people there made me feel welcome and a part of their fellowship. Because of this I decided to stay and worship with them and to become a member.*

*How do you go about becoming a member of the Salvation Army?*

*You have to be a committed Christian. I was invited to a series of recruits' classes which looked at what it means to be a* ***Salvationist*** *and what is expected of you.*

*What kind of work are you involved in throughout Northern Ireland?*

*To become a Salvation Army officer (minister) I had to study for two years at the William Booth Training College in London. When I finished studying and passed all my exams I was commissioned (ordained) and became an officer. Officers are given the title of Captain, just like a minister is called Reverend or a priest is called Father.*

*About every five years the Salvation Army moves its officers to new churches or areas of work. They might be asked to work in one of the Salvation Army's social service centres to care for people in need, in an office, or to work with children and young people. I could be asked to go anywhere in England or Ireland, or even abroad to any of the 111 countries the Salvation Army works in.* *[Continued overleaf]*

*My last appointment was as a minister at Carrickfergus corps. My wife Susan is also an officer and together we led Sunday meetings in the morning and evening. We would have singing, prayers and a short sermon. Many Salvation Army churches also have a brass band to provide the music.*

*During the week we visited members of the corps, especially elderly or sick people who were not able to get out and about very often. Sometimes we would visit together and sometimes separately.*

*During the week we organised a number of activities in our church hall. People from all over Carrickfergus would come along – not just those who worshipped in our church. The Salvation Army always tries to make sure everyone feels welcome.*

*Our weekly activities included a Bible study, and a friendship club for men and women where we sang, played games, had quizzes, or maybe listened to someone talking about a charity or something of interest. There was a social club for people over 60, and also a kids' club where children sang, listened to Bible stories, played games, did crafts, and were involved in lots of other activities.*

*Recently Susan and I were told that we would be moving from our church and would now be* ***chaplains*** *in the Salvation Army Thorndale Family Centre. This is a big building where families who have no home come and stay with us. They each have their own flat and there are lots of staff to help them with all sorts of problems.*

*As chaplains, it is our job to greet the families when they arrive and make them feel welcome. Some want us to pray with them and others just want a friendly chat. We organise lots of activities during the week for them. Every morning we have short prayers which staff also attend.*

*We have a coffee and toast morning every week when families come and get to know each other, hear a short thought based on a Bible verse, and pray together. We also have a kids' club once a week where we play games, draw pictures, sing and listen to Bible stories.*

*As chaplains, we know that God loves us and we want to share that with others. But because we are not working in a church we respect that some people don't want to know about God. We never force anyone to pray with us or listen to things about the Bible when they don't want to. Instead, we hope that by being friends with people they will see how happy we are, that God's love will shine through our lives, and that they will see a little of his love for them through us – without us even saying anything about him!*

*Sometimes we give families a Bible. Some families have asked us to dedicate their children – a service like a christening where we ask God to bless the child.*

*Sometimes we go with families if they have to meet important people or answer lots of questions. We just go so they don't feel alone. Other times something bad has happened to the families and they want to talk to someone about it, so we sit and listen.*

*How does the Salvation Army put Jesus' example of caring for others into practice today?*

*Jesus always took the time to listen to people and help them with their problems. He met both their physical and spiritual needs. He made a great impact on the people he helped and changed their lives for the better.*

*The Salvation Army tries not only to improve the quality of people's lives, but to show them the source of inner strength that comes from God. We try to show them that God values them and so they must value themselves. 'Belief in Action' sums up how the Salvation Army puts its Christian belief into practical action to help others.*

*What are the most difficult parts of your work?*

*Sometimes it's hard when people don't seem to want to learn more about God, and it's hard to know if they are listening to us or benefiting from our example. It's always lovely when people decide to become Christians. Sometimes when we don't see results it can be frustrating, but it's important always to remember the impact that God is having in someone's life – these results can't always be seen right away.*

*What is the most rewarding part of the work that you do?*

*It is very rewarding to see someone becoming a Christian. It is also wonderful to watch people realise what they're capable of and make progress in their lives.*

TPD Cit

Has Captain McFerran answered all your questions about the Salvation Army?

If you could talk to him, what else would you ask him?

Com MI TPD SM Cit

**Priority pyramid**

Draw a pyramid and give it the title 'The work of the Salvation Army'.

Fill in your pyramid, putting the things which you think are the most important at the top, and the least important at the bottom.

You could then report back to the rest of the class, explaining your choices.

TPD Cit

There is a saying, *"It's better to light one candle than to sit and curse the darkness."*

What do you think this saying means?

Com MI BC TPD WO Cit

In groups make a collage on the Salvation Army.

Your collage should give details about the background of the organisation and the work it is involved in today.

# The Church in the twentieth century

## Dietrich Bonhoeffer
(1906–1945)

Cit
PD

What would you be willing to die for?

Dietrich Bonhoeffer was born in Germany on 4 February 1906. He had a twin sister and six other brothers and sisters.

His father was a professor at Berlin University and many people thought that Dietrich would follow in his father's footsteps. However, early in life he decided to become a minister and his parents supported his decision.

Bonhoeffer studied **theology** at Berlin University and became a **Lutheran** pastor.

Many changes began to take place in Germany when Hitler came to power in 1933.

Bonhoeffer and some other ministers were unhappy with the control Hitler was taking of the Church in Germany.

They set up an organisation called the Pastors' Emergency League in opposition to the State Church which was controlled by the Nazis.

Bonhoeffer then spent some time in London as a pastor at two German-speaking Lutheran churches.

In 1934 the Pastors' Emergency League became an independent Church called the Confessing Church, and Bonhoeffer returned to Germany the following year to help to lead it. Because of pressure from the Nazis, the Church had to work in secret.

Bonhoeffer continued to oppose the Nazis. In 1939 he became involved with the **Resistance**. He joined a group who were planning to kill Hitler. Bonhoeffer was a courier, carrying important information and documents between the Allies and the Resistance.

The Nazis found out about this plan, and in March 1943 Bonhoeffer and the others were arrested and put in prison. He was hanged two years later.

Today you will find a statue of Dietrich Bonhoeffer, along with nine other twentieth-century martyrs, above the Great West Door of Westminster Abbey in London.

*The statue of Dietrich Bonhoeffer at Westminster Abbey*

Com
MI
TPD
WO
Cit
PD

Dietrich Bonhoeffer was a Christian, but he was involved in a plot to kill Hitler. Do his actions fit in with the teaching of Jesus?

*Blessed are the peacemakers ...*

*(Matthew 5:9)*

*... Love your enemies and pray for those who persecute you ...*

*(Matthew 5:44)*

*Put your sword back in its place ... for all who draw the sword will die by the sword.*

*(Matthew 26:52)*

On the other hand, the Bible teaches that Christians should defend the weak and fight against evil. There are also examples of violence in the Bible:

The Old Testament tells stories of God commanding people to go to war:

*"Proclaim this among the nations: Prepare for war!"*

*(Joel 3:9)*

This may suggest that God sometimes wants people to fight against their enemies.

*"Jesus ... overturned the tables of the money changers and the benches of those selling doves ..."*

*(Mark 11:15)*

Some Christians might say this incident shows that Jesus believed violence was acceptable in some circumstances.

In groups, discuss your opinions on this issue. After your discussion, each of you should choose one of the statements below and complete it:

1 I believe that Dietrich Bonhoeffer's actions were justified because ...

2 I believe that Dietrich Bonhoeffer's actions were not justified because ...

MI
TPD
PD

Find out about someone who has been martyred for their faith or beliefs.

Create a profile for them, outlining the important details of their life.

Include the following information:

| | | |
|---|---|---|
| Name | Religion | Date of death |
| Date of birth (if known) | Important life events | |
| Nationality | Reason for martyrdom | |

When you have learnt about this person, say what you think of them and what they did. Do you think they were right?

# Martin Luther King Jr
## (1929–1968)

Martin Mills/Getty Images Entertainment/Getty Images

*Martin Luther King in the late 1960s*

## LEADERS

We have lots of leaders in the world today – people who show they are leaders in writing, sport, politics, television, and so on.

Let's begin this section by looking closely at leaders.

Com
TPD

Call out the names of as many leaders as you can think of.

Either write them down yourself or your teacher will make a list.

Why are these people leaders?

Do you think they are all good leaders?

How do people become leaders? Sometimes it happens because of a vote. The MLAs and local councillors are examples of people who have been voted into leadership. They have been chosen by others.

To become a leader you need the qualities to do a good job.

TPD

**What makes a good leader?**

Draw a spider diagram like the one below.

Add qualities you think a leader should have.

One is filled in for you.

Different types of leaders might need different skills. For example, the leader of a school rugby or football team would need different skills from the manager of a local supermarket.

ICT
MI
BC
TPD

Choose a leader, eg the Prime Minister.

Find articles in newspapers and magazines or on the internet about this leader.

What do you learn about this person? Do you think they are a good leader or a bad leader?

Now draw a table with two columns labelled 'Positive' and 'Negative'. List the things you have found out about your leader in the right column.

## PREJUDICE

Com TPD WO Cit

What is prejudice?

How does it happen?

What can it lead to?

Think of some examples of things that have happened in this country because of prejudice.

Com ICT Ma MI BC TPD SM WO Cit

Carry out a survey on prejudice in your school.

First, make up questions for your survey.

For example, you could ask:

- Have you ever experienced prejudice?
- If the answer is "Yes", what type of prejudice have you experienced, eg prejudice because of age/religion/skin colour/clothes/hairstyle, etc?
- Do you think the school is doing enough to tackle prejudice?
- If you said "No", how do you think the school could tackle prejudice?

Ask ten people your questions.

When you have done this, think of a way to show your findings, eg in bar charts or pie charts.

Write a report to go along with your charts to explain them.

Com BC TPD WO Cit

In pairs, role-play an interview with a 14-year-old student who is experiencing prejudice in school.

First decide what the prejudice is about, then perform your role play.

## KING'S BACKGROUND

One Christian who fought **prejudice** was Martin Luther King Jr ('Jr' is short for 'Junior').

He was a black American Baptist pastor and lived at a time when it was not against the law to **discriminate** against black people.

He was born Michael Luther King in Atlanta, Georgia, but later changed his name to Martin after his father.

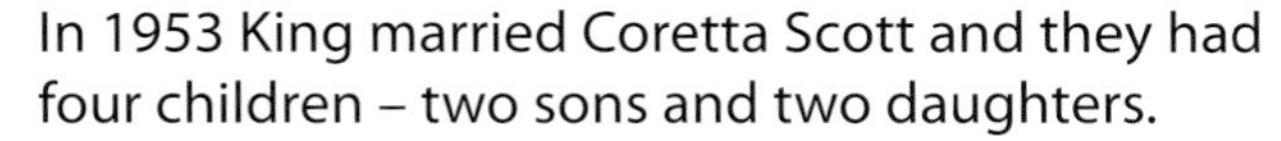

Com TPD WO PD

If you could have a different name which one would you choose?

Why choose that name?

If you had a different name would you feel like a different person?

Why are names so important to people?

In 1953 King married Coretta Scott and they had four children – two sons and two daughters.

He graduated from Boston University in 1955 and became a Baptist pastor.

*Martin Luther King and his wife Coretta in 1964*

## SEGREGATION

Even though **slavery** had been **abolished** in the United States (US) in 1865, most black people still lived in conditions that were a bit like slavery.

They earned half as much as white people; lived in **ghettos** and were often **segregated** in public; and they could not go to the same restaurants as white people or attend the same schools.

There were many other laws which segregated black people and white people from each other.

King believed that all humans were made in the likeness and image of God and should be treated equally. He felt that it was time to speak out against the treatment of black people.

King knew that violence was not the answer to the problem of **inequality** and so he began to teach black people that there was another way to protest.

Not all black people agreed with King's views. A **radical** group led by Malcolm X (a black Muslim leader) believed in using violence to achieve **equality** with white people.

## THE BUS BOYCOTT

King was pastor of Dexter Avenue Baptist Church in Montgomery, Alabama. In Montgomery, black and white people were segregated. For example, black people had to sit at the back of buses and were expected to give up their seats if white people wanted them.

On 1 December 1955 a black woman called Rosa Parks refused to give up her seat to a white man. She was arrested. Mrs Parks was not the first person to be arrested for this 'crime'. However, she was the first well-known person to be arrested in Montgomery – she was a secretary for the National Association for the Advancement of Colored People.

King and other community leaders decided it was time to do something. A meeting was held, with a huge crowd coming to Dexter Avenue Baptist Church to hear what King had to say. A bus **boycott** was organised and the Montgomery Improvement Association was founded. It was decided that the bus boycott would go on until the owners of the bus company changed their rules.

For 382 days black people across the city refused to get on buses. This meant that the city lost a lot of money, and on 13 November 1956 the US Supreme Court declared that it was against the law to separate black people from white people on buses.

Just a few days later, on 21 December, King shared the front seat of a bus with a white minister. The boycott had been a success.

Com
MI
BC
TPD
Cit

Imagine you are Rosa Parks.

Write a paragraph or two describing your thoughts and feelings on your bus journey.

How do you feel about the way you are being treated? What do you want to do about it?

## GANDHI

King's role model was Mohandas K Gandhi.

Gandhi was a practising **Hindu**, an Indian spiritual leader, and an independence campaigner. He was in favour of non-violence and practised this himself (see page 93 for more information).

King visited India in 1959 to study Gandhi's approach to non-violent protest.

In the same year, King resigned as pastor of his church to concentrate on his **civil rights** campaign for black people who were being treated unfairly.

## CAMPAIGNING

*Martin Luther King at a freedom rally in 1962*

In the following years, King kept on speaking against injustice even though he was stabbed, received many death threats, and had his home bombed.

He kept pointing out that Jesus said to love your enemies and pray for those who persecute you (see Luke 6:27). He believed that violence and hatred could be overcome by love and forgiveness.

Com
TPD
WO
Cit

What do you think of using non-violent methods to protest?

## PROTEST AND ARREST

In 1963, people all over the world heard about King when he was involved in a huge protest at Birmingham, Alabama. This protest was in support of fair hiring policies and ending segregation in department stores.

Rough treatment by police against the marchers made many more people around the world realise how black people were being treated.

King was arrested and spent eight days in jail.

After this, more jobs became available to black people and segregation was stopped in areas like toilets and fitting rooms.

## "I HAVE A DREAM"

Later that year, King led a peaceful civil rights march in Washington DC. He gave his famous speech, "I Have a Dream", at the Lincoln Memorial in front of over 200,000 people – both black and white.

He was named 'Man of the Year' by *Time* magazine.

Com Ma MI BC TPD SM WO Cit

King's dream could be called a *creed*. A creed is what people believe. It does not have to be religious belief – it can be belief in a set of ideas.

Ask ten people the following questions, then present your findings in a bar chart. You can think up your own questions if you wish.

- Do you think men and women should be paid the same wages?
- Do you think that health care should be free of charge?
- Do you think that rich countries should help poorer countries?
- Do you agree with smoking being banned in public places?
- Do you think drinking alcohol is a bad idea?
- Do you think people from different **ethnic minorities** are welcome in your community?

TPD Cit

King's famous speech describes his dream for the future in the US. Can you guess what kind of things he hoped for?

ICT MI TPD Cit

Now use the internet to find and read a copy of the full speech.

Slot the missing words into the extract from the speech below.

*"I have a dream that one day even the ________ of Mississippi, a desert state, sweltering with the heat of injustice, sweltering with the heat of ________, will be transformed into an oasis of freedom and ________.*

*I have a ________ that my four little children will one day live in a ________ where they will not be judged by the ________ of their skin but by the content of their character ...*

*I have a dream that one day ... all of God's children, black men and white men, Jews and ________, Protestants and ________, will be able to join hands and sing in the words of the old Negro spiritual, 'Free at ________! Free at last! Thank God ________, we are free at last!'"*

| | | |
|---|---|---|
| ***Almighty*** | ***color*** | ***Catholics*** |
| ***dream*** | ***Gentiles*** | ***last*** |
| ***nation*** | ***state*** | |
| ***justice*** | ***oppression*** | |

*Martin Luther King waving to the crowd after making his speech*

Com
ICT
BC
TPD
EfE
Cit
PD

What dreams do you have for your future?

Write about your dreams for the future. You can use pictures from newspapers, magazines or the internet to illustrate your dream.

Com
MI
BC
TPD
WO
Cit
PD

**The great Post-it challenge!**

Working in pairs, use Post-it Notes to list all the changes you think you will see in the world in your lifetime, eg economic, environmental, political and technological changes. Stick all the Post-it Notes on a sheet of A3 paper.

Think about whether these changes will be good or bad for the lives of people throughout the world.

Separate out the negative and positive Post-it Notes.

For all the negatives, think about what you can do about it. For all the positives, think about how you can contribute to it.

MI
BC
TPD
Cit

Research some changes that have taken place in the last 100 years – eg the fall of the Berlin Wall, the discovery of nuclear power, a man landing on the moon, and the partition of Ireland.

Have they affected people's lives?

If they have, how?

What changes would *you* like to see in the twenty-first century?

## NOBEL PEACE PRIZE

In 1964 King was awarded the Nobel Peace Prize, an award which is given to a person or people who have worked to encourage peace. At 35 he was the youngest ever to receive the award. He was also the second American and the third black man to receive it.

He gave the prize money to the civil rights movement in the US.

ICT
MI
Cit

In 1998 the Nobel Peace Prize was won by David Trimble and John Hume, politicians in Northern Ireland.

See what you can find out about the Nobel Prize, especially from its website (www.nobelprize.org).

Who is it named after?

Has anyone else in Northern Ireland ever received it?

## KING'S DEATH

On 4 April 1968 King was shot dead on the balcony of his motel room in Memphis, Tennessee. He was 39 years old. The man who shot him was James Earl Ray, a white American, but many people thought there might have been a **conspiracy**. His death led to violence in big cities in the US.

After his death, his life was unofficially remembered on 15 January, which was his birthday.

In 1986 Martin Luther King Day was observed as a national holiday in the US for the first time. It is held on the third Monday of each January.

Worldwide, he is one of the few leaders to be honoured with a national holiday.

There is a statue of King above the Great West Door of Westminster Abbey in London, along with nine other twentieth-century martyrs.

*The statue of Martin Luther King at Westminster Abbey*

Com
TPD
WO
Cit

If King was alive today, what do you think he would be doing?

What would he be speaking out against?

# Archbishop Oscar Romero (1917–1980)

*Map of Central America*

Oscar Romero was born into a poor family in El Salvador, Central America. When he was 12 years old, Romero became an apprentice carpenter, but he didn't feel that this was what God wanted for him.

In 1930 he got the opportunity to continue his education and spent seven years at the San Miguel **seminary**. He was eventually sent to Rome to study **theology** and became a priest in April 1942.

Because of the war going on in Europe at the time, Romero had to give up his studies. He returned to El Salvador and began working as a parish priest.

In 1977 Romero was made **Archbishop** of San Salvador (the capital of El Salvador).

At this time there was a civil war in the country. Poverty, social injustice, torture and murders had become normal for the people, and Romero was determined to speak out against all this.

He had been in his job only a short time when one of his priests was murdered. Romero demanded an investigation but the government ignored him.

Ordinary people liked Romero's message of social justice and they flocked to his Masses. However, attacks against the Church got worse, with priests being put in prison or sent away from the country. Romero did not take sides but asked the people to stop fighting and try to come to an agreement.

The day before Romero's death was a Sunday, and during his sermon he looked back on the events of the week before. He encouraged Salvadoran soldiers to disobey orders which went against God's laws and to *"stop the repression".*

This was the last straw for the army – the outspoken archbishop had gone too far. At 6.30 pm on 24 March 1980, Romero was murdered in front of the altar where he was celebrating Mass. He was shot through the heart by a single bullet.

Romero is one of the ten twentieth-century martyrs from across the world who have statues above the Great West Door of Westminster Abbey in London.

He is now undergoing **canonisation**.

*The statue of Archbishop Oscar Romero at Westminster Abbey*

*I am bound, as a pastor, by **divine** command to give my life for those whom I love … even those who are going to kill me.*

*(Archbishop Oscar Romero, 1980)*

These words appeared in a newspaper two weeks before Romero was shot.

Com TPD WO Cit

Do you think the Church today does enough to overcome poverty and social injustice?

# Corrie ten Boom (1892–1983)

*Corrie ten Boom in later life*

Com TPD WO Cit PD

You are going to learn about a woman who showed great bravery in a dangerous situation.

Can you think of any recent examples of people who have shown bravery?

Have you ever had to be brave?

## CORRIE'S BACKGROUND

Corrie ten Boom was born on 15 April 1892. Her parents were called Casper and Cornelia, she had a brother called Willem, and two sisters – Betsie and Nollie. The family owned a watch shop in the town of Haarlem in the Netherlands, and they lived over it. Their house was called the Beje.

MI

Find a map of the Netherlands and try to find Haarlem on it.

Many people in the town called Corrie's father 'Papa ten Boom'. He was a Christian and taught his children the importance of prayer and reading the Bible.

Corrie's family was very happy so it was a sad time for them when their mother took a stroke and died several years later.

Corrie became an assistant watchmaker in the shop, Nollie and Willem got married and left home, and Betsie took on the role of housekeeper.

As well as helping in the watch shop, Corrie worked with mentally handicapped children, teaching them Bible stories and verses.

## THE NAZIS

In January 1937 the ten Boom family celebrated the one hundredth anniversary of their watch shop, but the world as they knew it was about to change forever.

Adolf Hitler, the German dictator, was increasing in power and he wanted to wipe out the whole Jewish population as part of his plan to conquer Europe.

Every Jew in Europe was in great danger.

MI

Find out when Hitler came to power in Germany.

Com MI TPD WO Cit

Hitler thought that Jews were not as good as everyone else.

Does anyone today think that one race is not as good as another?

Do you think that any race has the right to destroy another one?

Why do you think this?

## THE SECOND WORLD WAR

The Second World War began when the German army invaded Czechoslovakia and Poland in 1939.

The Dutch Prime Minister broadcast a speech to his nation. He told them there was nothing to worry about, as he had assurances they would not be involved in the war.

He was wrong, because five hours later, on 10 May 1940, Germany attacked the Netherlands and took over the country.

When the Nazi soldiers first came to the Netherlands there was little change but soon they began to make new rules.

Dutch newspapers were closed down and all radios were confiscated. The ten Boom family hid a radio and listened to it secretly.

TPD Cit

Why do you think the Nazis closed the newspapers and confiscated the radios?

The Nazis took money, jewellery, cars and anything else of value from the Dutch people. There was a curfew – no one was allowed to be out of their home after a certain time each evening. Ration cards were needed to buy food.

The rules were even stricter for the Jews. For example, they were not allowed to work for the government, they couldn't go to public schools or universities, and they had to wear a yellow star with 'Jew' written in the centre of it.

Often Jewish shops and businesses were raided and destroyed by German soldiers. Sometimes Jews disappeared altogether. At the time, no one was sure what had happened to them, but we now know that around six million Jews in Europe were murdered by the Nazis.

## THE UNDERGROUND

One day in November 1941 some soldiers broke into a fur shop near the ten Boom's home. It was owned by a Jew named Mr Weil.

Corrie ran out into the street and saw the Nazi soldiers looting the shop. She brought Mr Weil to her home and later her brother Willem, who was involved with the Underground, helped the Weils escape from the Netherlands.

This was the beginning of Corrie's work with the Dutch Underground.

*A scene from The Hiding Place, a film made in 1975 about Corrie ten Boom and her family:*

*Papa ten Boom, his son, and nephew (dressed as a girl), smuggle a Jewish child out of Haarlem in a basket*

MI Cit

Find out what the Underground was and what role it played in the war.

Many Jews who needed help to escape from the Nazis came to the ten Boom house. The family knew that what they were doing was dangerous. They would be killed if they were found out, but they felt that they had to help.

The ten Booms were afraid of the Nazis taking them by surprise, so they fitted a warning buzzer and buttons to set it off throughout the house and shop.

When the buzzer went off, the Jews would rush to their hiding place.

The hiding place was a secret compartment that had been constructed by building a false wall in Corrie's bedroom.

*Corrie showing the hiding place. The Jews entered the secret room by the sliding panel at the bottom of the cupboard. The ten Boom house has been turned into a museum and visitors can go and see the hiding place for themselves.*

Com TPD WO

Look at the picture above.

How do you think it would have felt to have to hide in the secret room?

Com TPD WO

Imagine how the ten Boom family must have felt at this time in their lives.

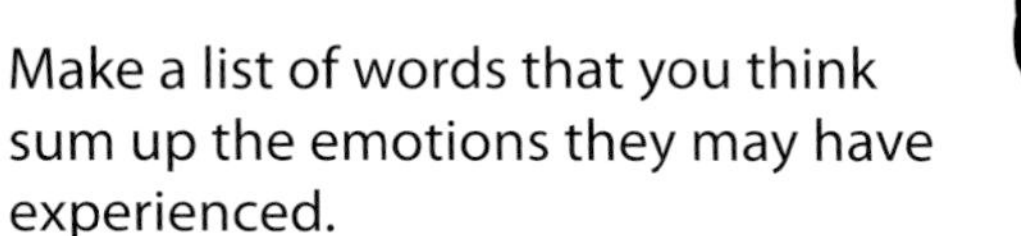

Make a list of words that you think sum up the emotions they may have experienced.

Now discuss your ideas with the rest of the class.

Com ICT MI BC TPD

A girl named Anne Frank and her family hid in a secret part of a building in Amsterdam for two years during the war. You may have heard of *The Diary of a Young Girl* by Anne Frank.

Find out more about Anne Frank and her diary.

Make a poster about it, using your computer.

## DISCOVERY

On 28 February 1944, Corrie was sick and had gone to bed. Betsie told Corrie that there was a Dutchman waiting downstairs to see her. He told Corrie that his wife had been arrested for helping the Jews and he needed 600 gilders (Dutch money) to get her released.

Corrie agreed to help him but she had just returned to bed when the buzzer sounded. All of the Jews clambered into the secret room just seconds before the door of the bedroom burst open and a member of the Gestapo (German secret police) rushed in.

The ten Booms later found out that the Dutchman had been working for the Gestapo.

The soldiers turned the ten Boom home upside down and questioned the family, but they couldn't find the secret room.

The ten Booms wouldn't say anything about the hidden Jews, so they were beaten up and arrested.

At its headquarters, the Gestapo offered to let Papa ten Boom go if he would promise not to cause any more trouble, but Corrie's father answered:

*If I go home today, tomorrow I will open my door again to any man in need who knocks.*

*(Corrie ten Boom, The Hiding Place, Hodder & Stoughton, 1976)*

Com TPD WO Cit PD

What do you think of Papa ten Boom's answer to the Gestapo?

How do you think he was feeling at the time?

Can you think of other examples of people who have stood up for their beliefs, no matter what?

Have you ever stood up for what you believe, in a difficult situation?

*Keystone/ Hulton Archive/Getty Images*

*Heinrich Himmler (left) with Adolf Hitler, 1941*

From 1934, the Gestapo was helped by a Nazi military organisation called the SS which was led by Heinrich Himmler.

It investigated anyone who was thought to be dangerous to the Nazi Party, and had the power to imprison people without trial.

It was also responsible for setting up and running **concentration camps**.

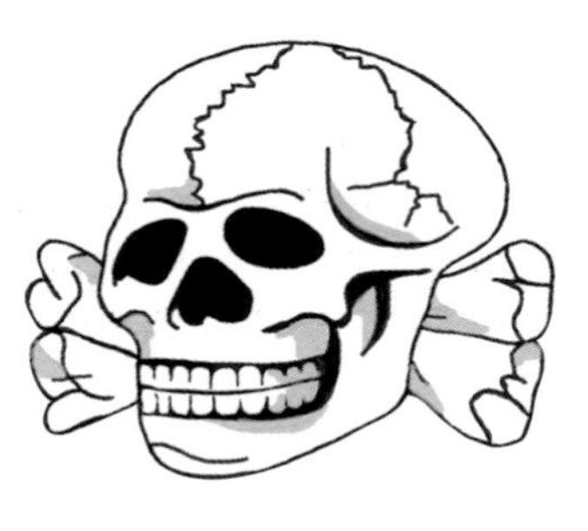

The SS used the death's-head (human skull) as one of its symbols.

Com TPD WO

Why do you think the SS used the death's head as one of its symbols?

## PRISON

The ten Boom family were taken to Scheveningen, a prison in the Hague. They were separated and this was the last time Corrie saw her father.

For two weeks Corrie shared a cell with four other women, but she was moved to a cell on her own because she was ill.

Corrie's cell was six steps long and two wide, and contained only a bed and a bucket. She stayed in this cell for about three months, and scratched a calendar on the wall to keep track of time.

One day Corrie got a package from her sister Nollie, who had been released. On impulse, Corrie peeled the stamp off and underneath it was written *"All the watches in your closet are safe."*

A short time later, Corrie got another letter from Nollie, telling her that Papa ten Boom was dead. He had died ten days after the arrest. Corrie scratched another date onto the wall under her calendar: *"March 9, 1944. Father. Released."*

TPD

What did Nollie's message mean?

Why did she choose this way of getting her message to Corrie?

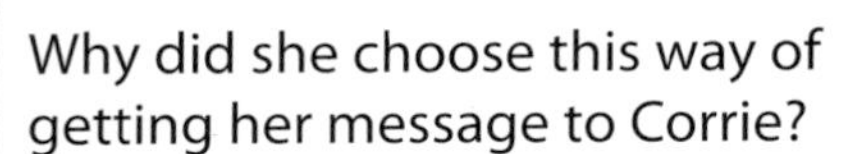

What do you think the words Corrie scratched on the wall meant?

Com BC TPD

Imagine that you are Corrie ten Boom at this difficult time in her life.

Pretend that you are having a conversation with God.

Write down what you think you would say to God and what he might say in return.

Later that month a lieutenant named Rahms started questioning Corrie about the Underground. Corrie told this man about the Bible and God's love.

He showed an interest and gradually began to tell her things. He told her about his family and how he was afraid for them as their town was being bombed every night.

He also told Corrie that he hated his job, and he helped her find the cell where Betsie was being kept.

In June, Corrie saw her sisters and brother again when they were all called to a reading of Papa ten Boom's will.

Her brother Willem had also been released, but wasn't very well. He died in 1945, from a disease he got in prison.

# RAVENSBRUCK

One day in June 1944, all of the prisoners were taken to a concentration camp at Vught, a town in the southern Netherlands. They lived and worked in terrible conditions there.

Later, in September, they were loaded onto cattle trucks and brought to Germany, to Ravensbruck concentration camp.

It was terrifying to see all the women being herded towards this place of death with its smoking chimneys and **crematorium**.

Would God really be with them in such a place? Corrie struggled with this issue – why would a God of love allow her to have come here?

Com
BC
TPD
WO

Look at the pictures on this page.

What is going on in these pictures?

How do they make you feel?

Have you any questions about what is happening in them?

*Scenes from The Hiding Place*

*Right: Betsie being forced onto the train for Ravensbruck*

*Below: Prisoners arriving at Ravensbruck*

Ravensbruck was worse than any other prison they had been in. They were packed into overcrowded barracks which were swarming with fleas.

They had to work for 11 hours a day, doing heavy manual labour, and the guards beat them with riding whips to make them work faster.

Corrie struggled with feelings of anger and hate towards the German guards, but her strong Christian faith and Betsie's support helped her.

She had managed to smuggle a Bible into the barracks, and she and Betsie shared their love for God with many prisoners.

Every evening, Corrie and Betsie would read the Bible to the other women, giving them hope for the future.

When Betsie became ill, she and Corrie talked a lot about what they would do when they were released.

Betsie said that they would set up a home for people who had been in concentration camps – a place where they could try to get over the awful things they had experienced. She described the large house they would use.

She told Corrie:

*We must tell people what we have learned here. We must tell them that there is no pit so deep that He is not deeper still.*

*(Corrie ten Boom, The Hiding Place)*

Betsie died in Ravensbruck shortly before Christmas in 1944.

Com TPD WO Cit

Do you think that Betsie ten Boom would have lived and died as she did if she had not believed in God?

TPD PD

Read Matthew 5:10–12.

What do you think Jesus meant?

Would these words be helpful to you if you were in an awful place?

TPD

CS Lewis, who wrote *The Chronicles of Narnia*, called this life *"Shadowlands"* in comparison to the afterlife.

What do you think he meant?

## FREEDOM

At morning roll call three days after Betsie's death, Corrie was brought to the administration building.

She was terrified – what was going to happen?

An officer there stamped a paper and gave it to Corrie. The paper said 'Certificate of Discharge'. She was free!

Corrie later found out that her release had been due to a mistake in paperwork.

Corrie went home to the Beje, but things weren't the same any more.

God had spared her life, so was there something special he wanted her to do?

Corrie soon remembered her sister's words: *"We must tell people, Corrie"* (Corrie ten Boom, *The Hiding Place).*

Com TPD WO

Look at the picture on this page.

How do you think Corrie felt as she left Ravensbruck?

*Scene from The Hiding Place: Corrie leaving Ravensbruck*

## TELLING HER STORY

It was time for Corrie to help others who had survived the horrors of the **Holocaust** and to tell her story of survival and faith in God.

She met a rich lady who let her use her mansion to set up a home for victims of the war. The mansion was exactly like the one Betsie had described.

The war ended in Europe in May 1945 and the home opened in June. It became a place where people could recover from the physical and emotional scars of their suffering.

Corrie also travelled a lot, telling people about her experiences. It was hard to go to Germany, but Corrie felt that God was helping her.

At a church service in Munich she came face-to-face with one of the guards from Ravensbruck. He held out his hand for her to shake, and at first Corrie didn't think she could do it, but she prayed and was able to take his hand and forgive him.

Com TPD WO PD

Do you think it was important for Corrie to forgive the guard? Why, or why not?

Have you ever had to forgive someone? Was it hard?

Corrie realised that people in Germany also needed help to recover from the war, so she took over a former concentration camp to set up another home. Again, it was just as Betsie had predicted.

In 1977, 33 years after her arrest, Corrie moved to California where she spent the rest of her life.

She died on 15 April 1983 – her ninety-first birthday.

She had visited over 60 countries and written many books, including *The Hiding Place* (1971), which was based on her experiences during the war.

This was later made into a film of the same name.

She was also named one of the Righteous Among the Nations (non-Jews who risked their lives to help Jews during the Holocaust).

A tree was planted in her honour in Jerusalem.

Com MI BC TPD Cit

Oskar Schindler is another person who has been named one of the Righteous Among the Nations.

A film called *Schindler's List* was made about him in 1993.

Find out more about Oskar Schindler and write a script for a short radio item about him.

MI TPD

Create a profile for the life of Corrie ten Boom, including all the important events, dates and people.

Com TPD WO Cit PD

Many people have found that reading about the life of Corrie ten Boon has helped them in their own lives.

Why do you think this is?

MI TPD PD

Find out about another person who put Jesus' teaching on forgiveness into practice in their life.

## Mother Teresa (1910–1997)

*Tim Graham/Tim Graham Photo Library/Getty Images*

*Mother Teresa in Calcutta, 1980*

Mother Teresa was born in the former Yugoslavia in 1910. She was the youngest of three children.

She felt God calling her when she was young. When she was 18 she left home to join the Sisters of Loreto – an Irish community of nuns that did a lot of work in India.

Mother Teresa trained for a short time in Dublin, before being sent to Calcutta, India, to teach in a high school. She was shocked by the poverty and suffering of the people. After teaching for 17 years, her superiors allowed her to leave the convent to work with the poor people in Calcutta.

She started a school in the slums to teach poor children, and also learned basic medicine so she could go into sick people's homes and treat them.

Before long, volunteers came and worked alongside Mother Teresa. They found people who were dying on the streets because they had been rejected by the local hospitals. The group rented a room so they could care for these people. This group became known as the Missionaries of Charity. They provided food, shelter, medicine and comfort to the sick and poor.

The group Mother Teresa started grew and grew, and today the Missionaries of Charity have branches all over the world. They help poor people, the homeless, alcoholics, **AIDS** sufferers, and refugees, among others.

Mother Teresa was given the Nobel Peace Prize in 1979. She continued helping people through her charity until she died in 1997, shortly after her eighty-seventh birthday. She is now undergoing **canonisation**.

Jesus said:

*... whatever you did for one of the least of these brothers of mine, you did for me.*

*(Matthew 25:40)*

TPD

1 Why do you think Mother Teresa wanted to work with poor and sick people?

2 Write down one way she followed the example of Jesus.

3 Mother Teresa was nicknamed the "Saint of the Gutter" and "Angel of Mercy". What do you think these names mean?

Do you think they are suitable names?

Com MI BC TPD SM Cit

Pick a charity that works with the poor anywhere in the world.

Now find out as much as you can about your charity. You could even write to them to learn more about the work they are doing.

Use your research to prepare a short presentation about them.

Com MI BC TPD Cit

Write a letter to the Prime Minister or a local politician saying what you think your country could do to help people around the world who do not have enough food and money or a place to live.

Com MI BC TPD WO Cit

In groups make a collage on Mother Teresa.

Your collage should show the work that she was involved in.

Mother Teresa and Princess Diana both died in the same week in 1997. Both were known for their caring attitude towards others.

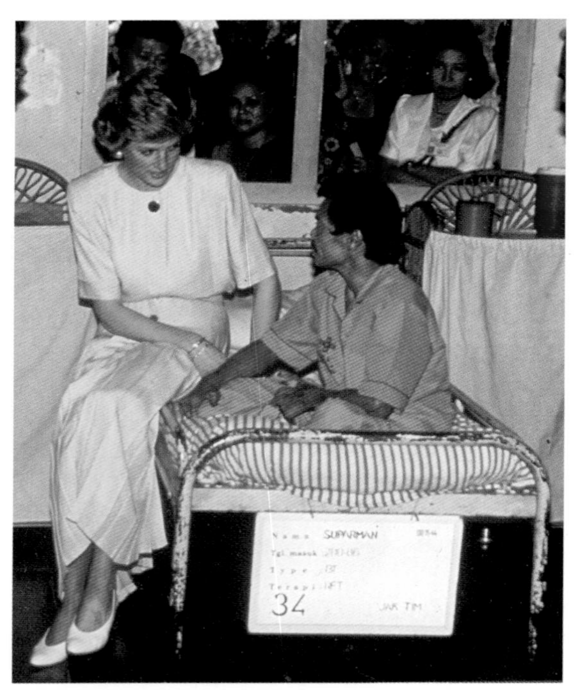

*Princess Diana at Sitanala Hospital, Indonesia, talking to a man suffering from leprosy*

Com TPD WO Cit

Have a class discussion about Mother Teresa and Princess Diana.

How were they similar and how were they different?

# Pope John Paul II (1920–2005)

Francois Lochon/Time Life Pictures/Getty Images

*Pope John Paul II in 1989*

TPD

Have you ever read the life story of, or seen a film about the life of, a famous person? Who was it? Did you learn anything interesting about them?

This is Pope John Paul II's coat of arms. The letter 'M' stands for Mary, the mother of Jesus. The keys represent those Jesus promised Peter.

TPD

Read Matthew 16:19 and write a short explanation of why keys were part of this coat of arms.

ICT BC TPD PD

Design your own coat of arms, representing you, your family, or your family name. You could use a computer to do this.

Decide:

- What images to use. Think about your likes, dislikes, hobbies, favourite pop groups, and so on.
- What colours to use

**George Best**

Northern Ireland has produced many famous people. One of the most well-known sportspeople was George Best – a footballer who died in 2005.

*George Best in 1970*

Central Press/Stringer/Hulton Archive/Getty Images

What does George Best have in common with Pope John Paul II, who also died in 2005?

- Both were keen footballers.
- Both have had airports named after them in their home countries.
- Both brought their home countries honour and glory.

**Pope John Paul II fact file**

He was the third longest-serving pope ever.

He was the first Polish pope.

He was good at his school work, skiing and football.

He was an honorary member of FC Barcelona.

His life was portrayed in a Marvel comic in 1983.

An airport was named after him in Balice, Poland – John Paul II International Airport.

After finishing high school, he enrolled in drama school because his first ambition was to be an actor.

He learnt Spanish after he became pope in 1978.

In 1994, *Time* magazine named him 'Man of the Year'.

## THE FIRST BISHOP OF ROME

MI

Read Matthew 16:13–20.

At Caesarea Philippi, Jesus gave his disciple Simon a new name. What was this new name?

This change of name was very significant because it means 'rock'. The Catholic Church believes that Simon was the rock on which the Church was built. He was the first **Bishop** of Rome and was succeeded by other bishops or **popes**. According to the Catholic Church, each pope inherits the power and authority first given to Peter by Jesus.

Com
TPD
WO

In 1985 Pope John Paul II called young people to join him for the first World Youth Day celebration in Rome. He held this event every year for as long as he was pope.

With a partner, look at what he said to young people. What was he asking them to do?

*It is Jesus who stirs in you the desire to do something great with your lives, the will to follow an ideal, the refusal to allow yourselves to be ground down by mediocrity ...*

*(World Youth Day, 2000)*

*Dear young people, the Church needs genuine witnesses for the new evangelisation: men and women whose lives have been transformed by meeting with Jesus, men and women who are capable of communicating this experience to others. The Church needs saints. All are called to holiness, and holy people alone can renew humanity.*

*(World Youth Day, 2004 )*

## POPE JOHN PAUL II'S BACKGROUND

Pope John Paul II was born Karol Jósef Wojtyla in Poland on 18 May 1920. His mother died when he was nine, his older brother died when he was 12, and his father died when he was 20. So by the time Wojtyla was 21, he was the only surviving member of his family.

He went to university but had to go to work when his university was closed by the Nazis. When the Second World War ended he continued his studies.

## BECOMING A PRIEST

There were three main events in his life as a young man that made Wojtyla choose to become a priest:

1. He was friends with a tailor in Kraków called Jan Tyranowski, who introduced him to the writings of Saint John.
2. One day he was knocked down by a tram when crossing a street and fractured his skull. The doctors thought it was unlikely that he would live. When he was in hospital he felt a powerful call to the priesthood but fought it off.
3. A few months later he was nearly crushed to death by a lorry.

## BECOMING POPE

By 1942 Wojtyla was studying for the priesthood and he became a priest in 1946. In 1978, at the age of 58, he was elected leader of the Catholic Church.

He was the 264$^{th}$ pope, the first Polish pope and the first non-Italian pope since the sixteenth century. He took the name John Paul II.

## TRAVEL

Pope John Paul II travelled around the world. He went to 129 countries in 104 trips outside Italy, including seven to the United States (US). This earned him the nickname "the globetrotting Pope".

He spoke many languages, including Spanish, German, French, Russian and English.

David Lees/Time & Life Pictures/Getty Images

*Pope John Paul II's first public appearance after his election, Vatican City, 16 October 1978*

Com TPD WO

Look at the picture above.

What do you see?

How do you think Pope John Paul II was feeling at the moment this picture was taken?

Pope John Paul II visited Ireland in 1979. This was the first time a pope had visited the country. He was flown to Phoenix Park in Dublin where he celebrated Mass in front of over one million people – nearly a third of the Republic of Ireland's entire population at that time.

He also visited the shrine at Knock where local people claimed to have had visions of Mary over 100 years ago. In Drogheda, he spoke in front of around a quarter of a million people, and called for peace in Northern Ireland, asking those involved in violence *"to turn away from the path of violence and to return to the way of peace".*

He wanted to visit Armagh but these plans were called off because of events of the Troubles in Northern Ireland.

After his visit to Ireland, Pope John Paul II toured the US.

## ASSASSINATION ATTEMPT

In May 1981 Pope John Paul II was almost killed. Leaning out of his jeep as it was circling Saint Peter's Square in Rome, he was shot and seriously wounded by a Turkish terrorist.

After a long recovery, he visited the man who tried to kill him and forgave him.

## DEATH

In 1992 Pope John Paul II was diagnosed with **Parkinson's disease**. He died on 2 April 2005 and was buried in the **crypt** underneath Saint Peter's **Basilica** in the Vatican. A white marble slab marks his grave.

Up to 10,000 visitors visit the crypt each day to pay their respects to him.

MI BC TPD

Try to find pictures of Pope John Paul II's funeral.

Where could you look?

What do the pictures tell you?

MI

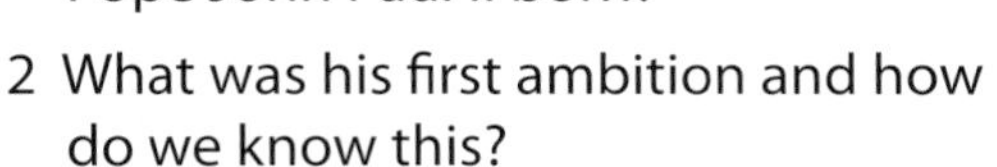

1 Where and when was Pope John Paul II born?

2 What was his first ambition and how do we know this?

3 What influenced him to become a priest?

4 How many countries did he travel to during his papacy? Name two of them.

5 How many languages could he speak?

6 What happened to him in 1981?

7 When did he die and where is he buried?

# ELECTION OF POPE BENEDICT XVI

*Pope Benedict XVI in 2005*

### 1 Cardinals summoned to Rome for a secret conclave

**Cardinals** meet together 15 to 20 days after the death of the pope. Those who are under 80 years old attend.

The new pope is elected from amongst the cardinals. They discuss who it should be and vote on it.

The voting takes place in secret. Nobody else knows exactly what is happening and the cardinals are not allowed to have any contact with the outside world, for example no mobile phones, and no messages or letters.

MI

Find out who are the cardinals in Ireland at the moment.

### 2 Voting ritual

The cardinals vote on the afternoon of the first day, then twice each morning and twice each afternoon. If no one has been elected after the first three voting sessions, then they may have a day of prayer before beginning again.

They write the name of their choice on a **ballot** that is folded in half. Taking it in turns, they hold their ballot in the air and then place it on a patten (plate).

### 3 Reaching a decision

A cardinal must get two-thirds of the vote in order to be elected. If this doesn't happen within a certain amount of time, a cardinal can be elected as long as they have a majority of votes.

When a decision has been made, the ballots are burned with chemicals to give white smoke. As well as the white smoke, the bells of Saint Peter's are rung to signal the election of a new pope.

### 4 New pope announced

When a pope has been elected he is asked if he accepts the job. If he does, he is then asked to announce his choice of name.

The new pope changes into white **vestments** (cardinals wear red while voting) and returns to the Sistine Chapel where the cardinals offer a sign of obedience.

The new pope then gives his blessing from the balcony of Saint Peter's to the people gathered there. He is officially admitted into his new position during a Mass a few days later.

BC
TPD

Draw pictures to represent each stage of electing a new pope.

BC
TPD

Imagine the Pope is visiting your area – the first time a pope has ever visited!

He is coming to your school and your class will be allowed to have a ten-minute audience with him.

What questions would you ask him, bearing in mind he will only have time to answer a few?

How do you think you would feel about asking the Pope questions?

ICT
MI
TPD

Use the internet to find out some information about the present Pope, eg what country he comes from and when he became a priest.

# The Church today

## Vocation

TPD
EfE
PD

What do you want to do when you grow up?

Own a house?

Have a good job?

Go to Barbados for your holidays?

Have plenty of 'bling'?

Get married?

Play football for Northern Ireland?

Have a sports car?

Go to university?

What would you do if you were asked to put someone or something else before your ambitions?

Could you?

And would you?

In this section you will learn about Christians who practise their faith in local and global communities – people who have put the needs of others first, before their own ambitions.

TPD

Can you think of some examples of people like this?

Christians believe that God has a purpose for every person which includes using their talents. Some believe that they are called to do a particular job. This is called a **vocation**. It comes from the Latin word '*vocare*' meaning 'to call'.

A call from God does not necessarily mean a flash of lightning or a booming voice. It might simply take the form of a strong feeling.

The word 'vocation' can mean several things:

1. Sometimes it is used to describe a religious calling, for example the call to be a minister, missionary or priest.
2. It can also be used to describe the 'caring professions', such as nursing and social work. These jobs are called vocations because they require a real concern for others. This may come because a person wants to serve God and others the way Jesus did.
3. However, Christians believe that everyone has a vocation. It is their responsibility to do their job to the best of their ability whatever it is, because this is what God wants them to do.

Com BC TPD WO EfE PD

Split into groups and put together a thought shower on the question *"Why work?"*

Then share your ideas with the rest of your class.

MI TPD EfE PD

Local newspapers like the *Belfast Telegraph*, *Newsletter* and *Irish News* publish job advertisements both on their websites and in print.

They publish certain jobs on certain days, eg the *Belfast Telegraph* publishes jobs in education every Tuesday.

Find a job advertisement for a job you think you would like. Explain why you have chosen it.

TPD PD

What things do you think would be the hardest to give up if you went to work in a very poor country?

Think about things like clean running water, money and safety.

# Maud Kells

## *Maud's background*

Maud Kells is from Cookstown, County Tyrone. She is a missionary with WEC International, and spends six months a year in the Democratic Republic of Congo.

Congo is a name shared by two countries next to each other in Central Africa.

One is known as the Democratic Republic of the Congo (DR Congo) and the other as the Republic of the Congo. The Republic of the Congo is the smaller of the two.

**WEC International**

WEC International is a nondenominational Christian organisation.

It has around 1,800 missionaries from many different countries. These missionaries work across the world with groups of people who don't yet know about Christianity. Their aim is to set up churches in these areas, which will keep on growing.

The organisation began as the Heart of Africa Mission, and was set up by two missionaries – Charles Thomas Studd and his wife Priscilla.

*Maud Kells wearing an African outfit. It is colourful because Africans like lots of colour and it is also political. The photos she is holding up show some of the people she works with and the activities she's involved with in DR Congo.*

Maud was brought up to go to church and Sunday school. She went to train as a nurse at the Royal Victoria Hospital in Belfast where she became involved in the Nurses' Christian Fellowship. She began to realise that there was more to Christianity than knowledge and reading the Bible.

Through the influence of Christian nurses and the Fellowship she says she came to know Christ and accepted him into her heart.

This made a big difference in her life because it gave her a focus. She asked God to show her what career she should follow.

Maud went to Edinburgh to train as a midwife. While she was there she attended a memorial service for missionaries who had been martyred in the Congo in 1965. She felt that she was being called by God to be a missionary. At first she didn't think she was good enough but promises in the Bible made her feel better about it.

DR Congo is one of the larger countries in the heart of Africa and the Equator runs through it. From 1971–1997 it was known as Zaire. It was once the personal property of King Leopold II of Belgium.

*Map of Africa showing DR Congo*

When Maud first went to DR Congo in 1968 nobody knew any English there. It had been a Belgian colony and so French was the main language. Swahili, an East African language, was also widely spoken. Maud polished up the French she had learnt in school and she had to learn Swahili.

## Mulita

For almost 20 years, Maud has been working in a little place in DR Congo called Mulita. Maud is the only missionary left in Mulita because others had to leave for various reasons.

When Maud arrived, both the primary and secondary schools in Mulita were closed down. There was a health centre and a Bible school. One of the things Maud did was to train midwives – many lives had been lost because there was no midwifery support.

Maud's work began with the hospital which was just a mud building. She started a building project to build a maternity unit with locally-made bricks and a concrete floor. A surgical ward was added and the operating theatre was rebuilt.

The school has now reopened. It is a mud hut where the children sit on logs. They have no textbooks but use exercise books to copy from the blackboard. Water is collected by the children from a spring.

## *Life in DR Congo*

The **infrastructure** in DR Congo is so poor that there is no postal service and the banking system has stopped working. Mobutu, who ruled the country until 1997, left his people with a poor standard of living.

There has been continuing trouble and rebellion in the country since it gained independence from Belgium in 1960. A rebellion in 1998 started a war involving six other nations.

It has been estimated that over three million people died between 1998 and 2003 because of the fighting, and there has been a lot of destruction.

The trouble in DR Congo has also affected Maud's work. Her Land Rover was stolen by rebels and she had to travel the 45 kilometres to the nearest town by bicycle. The hospital was left with no mattresses on the beds and no electricity. The airstrip which Maud uses became overgrown and had to be cleared.

## *Travelling to DR Congo*

Maud flies to Uganda where she buys medicines and equipment, as it is impossible to get things in DR Congo. She then hires a plane through the Missionary Aviation Fellowship (MAF) to Mulita.

## *AIDS*

**AIDS** is a problem throughout the world but especially in the developing world in places like DR Congo, where it has increased a lot because of the actions of the rebels involved in the fighting. It has been estimated that over one million people there are carrying the **HIV** virus.

Ma MI TPD PD

Look at the website www.worldvision.org.uk to find out more about HIV and AIDS.

See if you can find answers to the following questions:

- How many people in the world are affected by HIV and AIDS today?
- Which country has the highest number of AIDS victims?
- What age group has the biggest proportion of AIDS victims?
- What is World AIDS Day?

**AIDS statistics**

In 2006 there were:

- 39.5 million people living with HIV
- 4.3 million new infections
- 2.9 million AIDS-related deaths

*(UNAIDS/WHO, AIDS Epidemic Update, December 2006)*

Com MI BC TPD WO PD

Split into groups and put together a thought shower on the question *"How can we stop the spread of HIV and AIDS?"*

TPD

You have been given an opportunity to interview Maud Kells. Would any of the questions below help you to understand her vocation. Why, or why not?

- How often do you go back to Northern Ireland?
- Have you always been a Christian?
- Why are there so many poor people?
- What does the community of Cookstown think about what you do?
- Do you pray regularly?
- Why do you keep going back to DR Congo, even after bad things have happened, like having your Land Rover stolen?

# Dr Bill Woods

## *Bill's background*

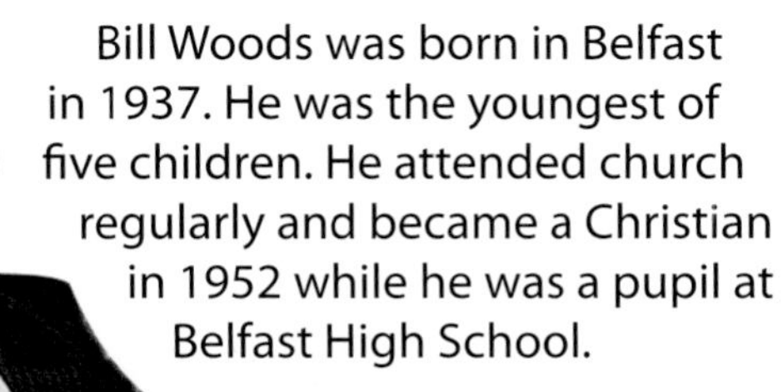

Bill Woods was born in Belfast in 1937. He was the youngest of five children. He attended church regularly and became a Christian in 1952 while he was a pupil at Belfast High School.

Bill's parents hoped he would become a teacher but he wanted to go to Bible college.

After leaving school, Bill took a job with Harry Ferguson Tyres in Belfast. He carried on going to church where he heard many missionaries speaking about their work. These people made him think very carefully about his future.

In January 1957 Bill went to the International Christian College in Glasgow. He studied there for two years.

While he was at college Bill heard Fred Orr, a missionary he knew, speak. Fred was a missionary in Brazil, South America. After college, Bill applied to work with the Acre **Gospel** Mission in Brazil.

**Acre and the Acre Gospel Mission**

Acre is a state in western Brazil. It is located within the Amazon rainforest and is well known for exporting rubber. The capital is Rio Branco.

The Acre Gospel Mission was set up in 1937 by Mr and Mrs WJ McComb. It is **interdenominational**, and works in four countries – Brazil, the Canary Islands, Portugal and Northern Ireland. You can find out more about the work it does on its website (www.acregospelmission.co.uk).

In the summer of 1959 Bill left Belfast for Liverpool and from there travelled on to Brazil on board the *SS Hubert*.

After six weeks the ship reached the Amazon (a river which flows through Brazil) and after another five days Bill arrived at Manaus, a city 1,000 miles upriver.

## *First days in Brazil*

Fred Orr and some others met Bill in Manaus. It was decided that Bill should travel with Fred to Lábrea and start learning Portuguese.

As Bill became better at speaking the language, he became aware of the people's needs and problems. He met his first leprosy victim, a man named Geraldo who had been thrown out of his family. Bill moved to Canutama in 1960.

Com
TPD
WO

When Bill arrived in Manaus there were only two cars in the city.

How do you think people travelled to the more remote parts of Brazil?

## *A change in direction*

In 1964 Bill came back to Belfast on his first **furlough**. This was the first time he had been home.

He used this time to attend a conference on leprosy and a three-month course on basic medicine at the Missionary School of Medicine (now Medical Services Ministries) in London.

He spent Christmas with his family and then returned to Brazil.

## *Medical training*

In 1968 Bill moved back to Manaus where he went to medical school. To make money to pay for his studies he taught English and built and sold houses.

When he finished his course in 1974, he was top of his class.

While in Manaus, Bill and a colleague called Franisco saw a new shoe demonstrated which would protect the deformed feet of leprosy victims. The sale of a house raised money for Franisco to go to the United States (US) where Dr Paul Brand showed him how these shoes could be made.

Bill left Manaus to spend two years in Rio de Janeiro studying ophthalmic (eye) surgery. After this he returned to Belfast on furlough and got more experience at the Royal Victoria Hospital.

ICT
MI
TPD
PD

Use the internet to do some research on leprosy.

Find out answers to these questions:

What is leprosy, and what happens to people who suffer from it?

When was it first discovered?

How is it treated?

Do many people still suffer from it?

## *The missionary doctor*

When Bill returned to Brazil, a lot of people wanted him to work for them. He could have worked for the government or with other missionaries.

He chose to work in Cruzeiro do Sul, a city in the state of Acre. Acre was known as "the leprosy state" and Cruzeiro do Sul had the largest number of leprosy cases in the state.

A portable microscope, sent from Northern Ireland, allowed Bill to do ophthalmic surgery, giving leprosy patients their sight back.

In 1982 Bill was asked to move to Rio Branco – the capital of Acre and its biggest city. He was to be in charge of the leprosy programme for all of Acre.

After improvements were made to the hospital in Rio Branco, Bill started to help leprosy victims living in isolated areas.

He was given permission to trial multidrug therapy (MDT). MDT was recommended by the World Health Organization (WHO) in 1981. Three drugs are put together and when the person with leprosy takes them they are cured.

## *The rewards*

Many people and organisations have recognised the work of Dr Bill Woods.

He has spoken to the International Leprosy Conference and has an award from the Brazilian College of **Dermatologists**.

The Brazilian Ministry of Health goes to him if it needs advice. He has also given help to the countries of Bolivia and Angola.

On 1 January 1997 Bill was awarded an OBE by the Queen.

MI
TPD
Cit

Find out what an OBE is.

Make a list of some people who have received one and why they received it.

## *An interview with Dr Bill Woods*

*Why did you decide to become a missionary?*

*At a missionary meeting I was one of many who said I would be willing to go if the Lord called me. I really did want to serve the Lord. Many of my friends from my church were going to Bible school and to the mission field. I attended missionary prayer meetings at the WEC headquarters in Belfast. All of this influenced me.*

*Why did you go to Brazil?*

*I knew Fred and Ina Orr quite well before they left for Brazil. Ina died on the first journey to Brazil – she never reached Lábrea where she was to begin learning Portuguese. The Lord used this to speak to me: "I looked for a man among them who would ... stand before me in the gap ..." (Ezekiel 22:30).*

*What made you want to become a missionary doctor?*

*It was the need around me. I lived for a long time in a town that was ten days' journey away from the nearest hospital or doctor.*

*A boy brought to me by his brothers, who was dying after a snake bite, told me he didn't want me to pray for him but to do something to save his life and ease his pain. But I had no medical training to help him. Then I met a little boy who was about seven. He had no feeling left in his hands because of untreated leprosy.*

*Describe your work as a missionary doctor.*

*Leprosy is treated with a combination of three drugs. Treatment lasts either six months or one year. We have teams of nurses, auxiliary [assisting] nurses and* ***paramedical*** *workers who help make diagnoses and give treatment.*

*We try to stop patients from becoming deformed and we have a surgeon who operates on people with deformities. We also have two workshops for making special shoes, boots and artificial legs for patients.*

*I have just come back from an annual science conference in Brazil. Last year I was the opening speaker because the leprosy programme in Acre was considered one of the most successful in the world. This meeting was held in one of the luxury hotels in Brasília – the capital of Brazil. All the international film stars and visiting presidents stay at the hotel, so I lapped it all up for a few days!* *[Continued overleaf]*

*During the next three weeks I'll be travelling on the Juruá River in the boat pictured on the left. This is so I can treat leprosy sufferers on the river.*

*Some days I'll be spending 10 or maybe 12 hours in an aluminum canoe, and I'll be wishing I was sitting in a comfortable chair without dozens of mosquitoes around my feet!*

*The boat will do perhaps three more journeys in 2007 to complete the treatment of the last 30 patients on this river.*

*This should be my last trip for the next while. A few years ago we had over 400 patients on treatment and the trip took three months to reach them all!*

*In 2007 I will turn 70 and will have to retire.*

*What have been your greatest rewards as a missionary?*

*I think my greatest contribution for the church work was helping a down-and-out alcoholic to become a pastor and preacher of the gospel. It was a long battle to rebuild his life.*

*I'm responsible for the government leprosy programme in the state of Acre. For the last 60 years Acre has had the highest number of leprosy cases in all of Brazil. A 1981 survey showed that for every 10,000 people in Acre, 105 people suffered from leprosy. But by March 2007 we hope the disease will be eliminated (gone) from the state.*

*Brazil had the highest number of leprosy cases in the world until 2005, and still has the highest number of new cases every year – around 80,000. But the good news is that the number of leprosy cases in Brazil has been reduced by 97%.*

*What is your favourite Bible verse?*

*James 4:17. When I feel I've done enough the verse tells me to do some more.*

*How can people in Northern Ireland support your work as a missionary?*

*People can pray and support the Acre Gospel Mission. It has a website and produces a newsletter.*

MI

Create a timeline for Dr Bill Woods, showing key events in his life.

Start in 1937, when he was born.

Com TPD WO

Do you think that what Jackie did was wise? Why, or why not?

Com BC TPD WO

**Useful objects**

A portable microscope sent from Northern Ireland was very useful to Dr Bill Woods' work.

Imagine that you are on a desert island. You have the object pictured below.

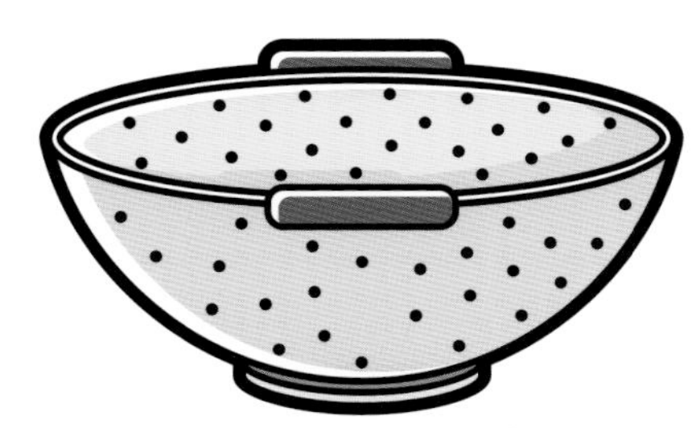

What could this object be useful for?

## Jackie Pullinger

In 1966 Jackie Pullinger gave up everything to work in a very dangerous part of the world.

Jackie decided when she was at Sunday school that she wanted to be a missionary, but when she was older she went to study at the Royal College of Music in London.

When she was 22 years old she felt that God was calling her to do something in the Far East.

She applied to many missionary groups but none of them would accept her. This was because they thought she was too young and didn't have the right experience or qualifications.

Jackie's minister advised her to go to Hong Kong anyway, so she did.

When Jackie arrived in Hong Kong she found a job teaching music at a primary school in the Walled City. The Walled City was a very lawless place where thousands of criminals and drug addicts lived.

At first Jackie wasn't sure why she was there but after a while she felt that God was letting her know his plan. She realised that she needed to help the people in a practical way, so she began working among the drug addicts in her neighbourhood.

Jackie had great success, and brought hope to people who thought there could be no hope. She opened up homes for drug addicts and with the help of friends formed the St Stephen's Society.

The St Stephen's Society has become one of the most successful drug rehabilitation organisations in the world and now also works in Thailand and the Philippines.

Com TPD WO PD

You've now learnt about some people who have a vocation.

What is the difference between having a vocation and doing a job?

BC TPD

How could your school support missionaries like Maud Kells, Dr Bill Woods and Jackie Pullinger? Draw up a list of suggestions.

MI BC TPD

Find out what an acrostic is. Then create an acrostic for the word 'vocation'.

Ingrid Bergman starring in the 1958 Hollywood movie about Gladys Aylward's life – *The Inn of the Sixth Happiness*

Gladys Aylward (1902–1970) is another example of a person who had a vocation.

Gladys, a London parlour maid, believed that God was calling her to be a missionary in China. When she was 26 she began a training course at the China Inland Mission, but failed her first term. Then Gladys decided to go to China on her own.

She worked in two jobs to pay for her train fare. In 1932 she began her journey. When she left England she had little more than her passport, tickets, a small amount in traveller's cheques, and ninepence in cash, which is less than 5p nowadays!

When she arrived in China she worked with an elderly missionary called Jeannie Lawson. Together they set up an inn for mule drivers, where the drivers could rest and listen to Bible stories. Mrs Lawson died a year later.

Gladys didn't give up when people were against her. Her Christian example and caring nature eventually led to people respecting and admiring her. Many people became Christians because of her work.

Gladys also led over 100 children to safety over the mountains when Japanese forces invaded China.

The local Chinese people called Gladys '*Ai-weh-deh*' (meaning 'virtuous one').

Com
TPD
WO

Think about what you pack when you are going away.

Could you go on a long journey with as little as Gladys Aylward?

Why could you, or why could you not?

Com
ICT
MI
BC
TPD
SM

Find out about someone in your local community who has a vocation.

You will have to think about where you could find information. You could try:

- Your teacher
- The local and school libraries
- The internet
- People you might know such as a pastor, minister, priest, nun or even a missionary
- Places of religious worship, eg a church

Use what you have learnt in this section to help you think of questions or headings to structure your research.

You could produce a written report, or you could create a poster.

## SUNDAY – A DAY FOR WORK?

Having a job means working many hours and sometimes even seven days a week.

In Northern Ireland large stores such as Marks & Spencer are allowed to open for five hours on a Sunday, usually meaning that they trade from 1.00 pm to 6.00 pm. They often open half an hour beforehand to allow people to browse. Many businesses remain closed on a Sunday. In the rest of the United Kingdom (UK) stores can open for six hours, so they often open at 11 am.

Many Christians think that Sunday should be a day of rest from work for the following reasons:

1. Genesis, the first book in the Bible, says that God created the world in six days and rested on the seventh day. So many Christians believe that there should be one day of rest in every seven days.
2. The fourth commandment says that people must keep the Sabbath day holy. For Jews, this is a Saturday. Christians have Sunday as a holy day.
3. The Bible says that Jesus observed the Sabbath so Christians believe that they should follow his example by having a holy day.
4. The Bible says that Jesus rose from the dead on a Sunday and so Christians remember his resurrection by having their day of respect and rest on Sundays.

Com MI BC TPD WO PD

Have a class debate.

The motion (issue being debated) is *"This house believes shops in Northern Ireland should not be allowed to open on a Sunday."*

## THE WORLD OF WORK

Com MI TPD EfE

Choose someone you know, such as a family member or a neighbour and find out more about their job.

Find out what you need for this job, eg qualifications needed, hours worked, pay, holidays, and place of work.

What do people in this job do?

Com TPD WO

Study the pictures below.

What do you see?

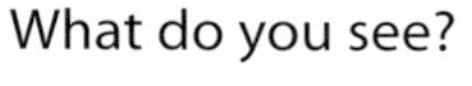

What do they tell you about the world of work?

TPD EfE PD

**My future!**

You have learnt in this section how some people believe God has asked them to become missionaries. For Dr Bill Woods, talks given by other people were also very important when he was deciding what to do.

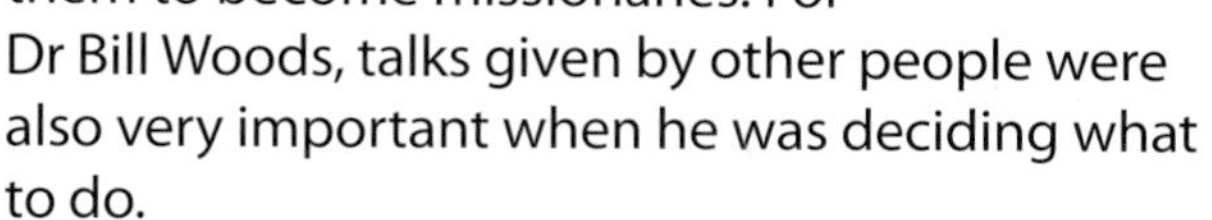

What about *your* future career? What job do you hope to have?

Why are you thinking you might do this? Is there anything influencing you at the moment?

Draw a tree like the one below and label it:

- Roots – people or things which are influencing your choice of career, eg family, careers teacher
- Trunk – your strengths, eg if you are a good listener
- Branches – your achievements, eg Grade 3 piano, but other things too, even if there isn't an exam in it
- Sun – hopes for the future, eg the job you're aiming for, or any other hopes you have

# Tolerance and harmony

Throughout the world many people find life difficult because they are persecuted because of their race, age, religion or gender.

MI
TPD
Cit

Have you ever heard the words *anti-Semitism* and *Islamophobia*?

Find out what they mean.

Now list some examples of anti-Semitism and Islamophobia. Try to think of things happening today as well as in the past.

MI
TPD
Cit

Copy the following words into your notebook and write the correct meaning beside each one. Can you think of an example of each from films or TV programmes?

**Words**

a Stereotype

b Prejudice

c Discrimination

d Racism

e Ageism

f Sexism

**Meanings**

1 Prejudice in action

2 Prejudging someone without really knowing them

3 Treating people differently because of their gender

4 Treating people differently because of their colour, culture or ethnic origin

5 The idea that people in a certain group are all the same

6 Treating people differently because of their age

TPD
Cit
PD

Think about a time when you felt you were not shown enough respect.

What happened?

How did you feel?

How do you feel thinking about it now?

Why do you think this happened?

Now think about a time when you saw someone else being shown a lack of respect.

How do you think they felt? How could you tell?

Do you know how they feel now about what happened?

Why do you think they were treated badly?

Was there anything you could have done to help?

## RELIGIOUS PREJUDICE

Com
TPD
WO
Cit

Religion often causes conflict.

Why do you think this is?

Understanding other religions and accepting that not everyone thinks the same way can help put a stop to religious **prejudice**.

TPD
Cit

Read the following Bible passages about prejudice:

Mark 10:13–14

John 4:1–9

Does anything happen today that is a bit like what happened in these stories?

Pick one of these stories and draw a cartoon strip of it.

## RACIAL PREJUDICE

Com
TPD
WO
Cit

Have a look at the following statements:

They're foreigners and you can't trust them.

You should smell their cooking – it would put you off your own.

I've worked hard to get where I am. Why should they push in?

The street doesn't seem the same since they arrived.

They talk too fast and make a lot of noise.

Talk about each one. What makes people say these things?

Do you think any of the statements are reasonable? Why, or why not?

ICT
MI
Cit

**Web search**

Look at the websites below and list some of the things these organisations are doing to try and end racism. Is there anything you could get involved in?

Commission for Racial **Equality** – www.cre.gov.uk

Show Racism the Red Card – www.srtrc.org

## TOGETHER IN HARMONY

There are many people and groups who work together to support the right of every human being to live in harmony and peace, regardless of skin colour, nationality or religious belief.

We've already looked at a twentieth-century figure who fought for people of all colours to be treated the same – Martin Luther King.

Now let's look at one man who is still doing this in the twenty-first century.

## Archbishop Desmond Tutu

*Archbishop Desmond Tutu in 2004*

Desmond Tutu was born on 7 October 1931 in Klerksdorp, Transvaal, South Africa. Klerksdorp is a small gold-mining town about 120 miles from Johannesburg, which the richest city in South Africa. His family, like all other black people in South Africa at the time, had very little money.

Tutu became known worldwide during the 1980s for being against **apartheid**.

### *Apartheid In South Africa (1948–1994)*

An election was held in 1948 and the National Party was voted into power by white South Africans who were the only ones allowed to vote.

This party was openly racist. It called for apartheid, which literally means 'apart-hood'. It began to introduce extreme anti-black policies:

1. Everyone was classified according to their race. The four main categories were White, Black, Indian and Coloured.
2. **Mixed marriages** were not allowed.
3. Black people and white people had to live in different areas.

*(Continued overleaf)*

4 Black people and white people had to use separate amenities (eg toilets, hospitals, beaches, parks and buses). Signs like the one below were put up across the country.

5 Black people weren't educated as well as white people.

6 Separate universities were set up for black people.

7 Black people weren't allowed to travel freely throughout the country without a pass.

8 Black people didn't have the same political rights as white people.

*Sign on a beach in Durban, South Africa, in 1989*

Com BC TPD WO Cit

Look at the picture above.

What do you see?

How does it make you feel?

Do you have any questions about it?

## *Tutu's education*

Tutu wanted to be a doctor but his parents couldn't afford this. So instead in 1954 he became a teacher like his father.

He resigned three years later after deciding to study **theology** instead. He became an **Anglican** priest in 1960. Between 1962 and 1966 he studied theology again, at King's College in London.

## *Tutu's career*

From 1967–1972 Tutu taught theology in South Africa. Then he spent three years in London working for the World Council of Churches – an international and nondenominational Christian group.

He returned to South Africa in 1976, and became **Bishop** of Lesotho the following year.

MI

Find Lesotho on a map.

What do you notice about it?

## *Tutu's achievements*

Tutu achieved a number of firsts as a black man. Find out about these by completing the next activity.

Ma

Can you work out the maths calculations to find the correct dates?

In *(459 × 4) +139* he was appointed Dean of Saint Mary's Cathedral in Johannesburg.

He became the General Secretary of the South African Council of Churches in *((1,215 + 1,521) ÷ 3) + 1,066.*

He became Bishop of Johannesburg in *(25,000 ÷ 10) – 515.*

In *(130 × 15) + 36* he was elected **Archbishop** of Cape Town. This made him head of the Anglican Church in South Africa and leader of the country's 1.6 million Anglicans.

## *Tutu's family*

Tutu married Leah Nomalizo Shenxane in 1955 and they now have four children.

## *Tutu's politics*

Tutu was General Secretary of the South African Council of Churches from 1978 until 1985. It was during this time that he became very well known in South Africa and around the world. He spoke out against the injustices of the apartheid system.

For several years he wasn't allowed a passport to travel abroad, but in 1982 international pressure made the South African government change its mind.

## *Nobel Peace Prize*

Tutu received the Nobel Peace Prize in 1984 because he had worked so hard for racial justice in South Africa.

There was a bomb scare at the award ceremony. Police had to clear everyone out of the building and search it. The bomb scare turned out to be a hoax and nothing was found.

In his speech, Tutu talked about the injustices taking place in South Africa under apartheid. He encouraged people across the world to work together for peace and justice.

MI TPD

What did Tutu set up with the prize money?

To find the answer, begin with the first letter below and then write down every third letter after that.

s e e o y t u h g t m n h i u e f g r k j n j k a g h f v
b r i o i k l c e r a x c n e r r s d e j k f u i u r t g q w
e a s e s d s c v c b n h c v o j k l y u a e r r d f s j k
h d f i z x p o p f t y u d f n i o d

Can you find out more about this?

TPD PD

Many awards are handed out today, like the BBC Sports Personality of the Year, the Ryder Cup, and the Oscars. Can you think of other examples?

Tutu was awarded the Nobel Peace Prize. In Northern Ireland, politicians John Hume and David Trimble have also received it (see page 63).

Have you ever received praise for something you have done, or an award for something?

If you have, how did it feel?

How do you think it would feel to receive a really big award like the Nobel Prize?

Com BC TPD Cit PD

Read this extract from Tutu's speech at the award ceremony:

*"There is no peace in South Africa. There is no peace because there is no justice ... [We need to work] so that all of God's children, our brothers and sisters, members of our one human family, all will enjoy basic human rights, the right to a fulfilled life, the right of movement, of work, the freedom to be fully human ... Let us work to be peacemakers ... God calls us to be fellow workers with him, so that we can extend his kingdom of shalom, of justice, of goodness, of compassion, of caring, of sharing, of laughter, joy and* ***reconciliation*** *..."*

Now imagine you have received an award and write your own speech. Include ways you think we can make a better world for everyone.

## *Truth and reconciliation*

In 1995 Nelson Mandela, the President of South Africa, appointed Tutu to chair South Africa's Truth and Reconciliation Commission.

This Commission looked into possible **human rights** abuses during the time of apartheid. The Commission also brought in housing, education, and economic plans to help black people.

**Nelson Mandela**

Nelson Mandela is a black South African who was born in 1918. He was in prison between 1962 and 1990 because he used violence against the National Party, which was ruling South Africa at the time.

When he was released he worked with the president, de Klerk, to end apartheid.

He won the Nobel Peace Prize in 1993 and became President of South Africa in 1994. He retired from politics in 1999.

His **autobiography**, *Long Walk to Freedom*, was published in 1994.

BC TPD

What other things would you like to know about Nelson Mandela?

How could you get the answers to your questions?

## *Tutu's retirement*

Tutu retired in June 1996, but was then named Archbishop Emeritus, which meant he could keep on calling himself Archbishop even though he had retired.

He holds **honorary degrees** from many universities, including Harvard, Oxford, Cambridge, Yale, Aberdeen and Sydney. He has received many prizes and awards as well as the Nobel Peace Prize, such as the Archbishop of Canterbury's Award for Outstanding Service to the Anglican Communion, and the Martin Luther King Jr Non-violent Peace Prize.

Every year, Queen's University Belfast and the University of Ulster award honorary degrees.

Peter Canavan, Gaelic player who captained Tyrone when they won the All-Ireland Championship in 2003, received an honorary degree in 2003 because of his commitment to sport.

David Humphreys, Irish international rugby player, also received an honorary degree in 2002 for services to sport.

The Archbishop of Canterbury is the leader of the Anglican Church in Great Britain. Can you find out who is the Archbishop now?

In Northern Ireland, Anglicans are known as members of the Church of Ireland. They are led by the Archbishop of Armagh.

Com TPD SM WO Cit PD

In December 2006 Tutu was interviewed on the BBC's Heaven and Earth show. He was asked what his New Year's resolution would be for 2007.

He said *"Peace, peace, peace".*

Every year people make New Year's resolutions

What kind of resolutions do they make?

Have you ever made any?

Did you manage to keep them?

If not, why not?

What could make Tutu's resolution fail?

Com TPD SM Cit

### Spectrum debate

Tutu became involved in politics during his ministry. Some people feel that Christians should be involved in politics so that they can be a good influence. Others disagree.

What do you think?

*"Christians should not be involved in politics."*

Imagine there is a line down the centre of your classroom. One end represents complete agreement with the statement above, and the other end represents complete disagreement.

Think about your opinion on the statement and then take a position along the line.

Your teacher will ask you why you've chosen that position.

After listening to what your classmates have to say, you can change your position on the line, but be ready to explain why!

MI

### True or false?

Write out the following statements again, correcting any that are false.

Tutu was born in Peebles, Scotland.

He was a teacher before he became a priest.

Tutu studied theology in London in the 1960s.

He married Gladys in 1966 and they have five children.

In 1976 Tutu became Bishop of Lesotho.

In 1982 he was awarded an Oscar.

He became head of the Anglican Church in South Africa in 1975.

President Nelson Mandela of South Africa made Tutu Chair of the Truth and Reconciliation Commission in 1995.

He was awarded the Martin Luther King Jr Non-violent Peace Prize.

Tutu retired in May 1996.

# GANDHI

Mohandas K Gandhi (1869–1948) is often known as Mahatma Gandhi. He is an important figure for **Hindus**. Nearly every town and village in India has a statue or picture of him.

He believed in non-violence and thought that all of the big world religions had some truth in them.

Gandhi was born in Gujarat, India, and trained as a lawyer in London. In 1893 he was offered a job in South Africa.

While he was studying in London, he had not felt any **prejudice** because of his race. However, while working as a lawyer in South Africa, Gandhi experienced racism and prejudice for himself. This would change his life.

MI

Fill in the blanks with the words from the box below:

He was asked to take off his ________ in court. Gandhi ________ and left the courtroom.

A short time later, he was travelling on a train with a ________ ticket. A white traveller ________ and Gandhi was ordered to ________ the first-class compartment. When he refused he was thrown off the train.

Two days later he was forced to sit outside the coach box of a ________, while the white passengers travelled ________. The final insult came when Gandhi was ordered to sit on the footboard so that the man in charge of the stagecoach could sit down for a ________. Gandhi wouldn't give up his seat so the man ________ him.

Gandhi was also ________ from many hotels.

| | | |
|---|---|---|
| *complained* | *smoke* | *leave* |
| *turban* | *first-class* | *barred* |
| *inside* | *beat* | |
| *refused* | *stagecoach* | |

TPD

Copy out and complete the spider diagram to show how Gandhi may have felt in the railway carriage.

Add as many legs as you can to the spider.

Gandhi is told to leave the carriage

Sad

Experiences like those on the train and the stagecoach were life-changing for Gandhi. They made him want to fight against injustice. He decided to stay in South Africa and try to improve conditions for Indians living there.

In 1915 he returned to India.

Com TPD WO PD

Have you had any experiences which have changed your life, or maybe changed how you felt about something or someone?

Gandhi hated violence and thought that it created more problems than it solved. In January 1948 he began a **fast** to protest again violence between Hindus and Muslims in India. He refused to eat until six days later when the opposing leaders agreed to stop fighting.

Some Hindus were angry with Gandhi because he tried to bring together people from different religious groups. On 30 January 1948, Gandhi was murdered by a Hindu **fanatic** called Godse.

Gandhi has inspired many people throughout the world, including Nelson Mandela and Martin Luther King. His birthday on 2 October is a national holiday in India called Gandhi Jayanti.

You can find out more about the Hindu faith in *Local People, Global Faiths: Sikhs, Jews and Hindus in Northern Ireland* by James Nelson and Norman Richardson (Colourpoint Books, 2005).

# THE LOCAL COMMUNITY

BC TPD Cit

In this book, you have looked at the lives of people who have worked for peace in different parts of the world.

Now think about your own local community.

What do you know about groups of people from other countries or belonging to different faiths?

How could you find out more?

Since 2004 many new countries have joined the European Union (EU). This makes it easier for people to live and work in new places.

In any town or village in Northern Ireland you will find people of different nationalities and religions.

In Portadown and Dungannon there is a large Portuguese community. Shops like Tesco have signs in Portuguese.

Northern Ireland also has a growing Polish community. In Fermanagh Masses are sometimes held in Polish in the Convent Chapel in Enniskillen. The *Impartial Reporter* and the *Fermanagh Herald*, the two leading Fermanagh weekly papers, have columns written in Polish by Polish people.

*A Polish shop in Belmore Street, Enniskillen*

Com BC TPD WO Cit

Is there anyone in your class who is from a **minority** group? If so, ask this person how they feel about living here. What do they like or not like?

Can you think of ways your local community could welcome and help people of other nationalities or faiths?

TPD Cit PD

Imagine moving to a new country. What do you think would be the most difficult thing for you?

Here are some examples:

- Finding your way around
- Making new friends
- People being unfriendly because you come from a different country
- The different food
- Not understanding what people say because of the language
- Not being able to find a job because of prejudice
- People not understanding your lifestyle because you are from a different culture

Could you add other things to this list?

Com TPD WO Cit

**Snowballing**

Think about the following question: *"What can people do to help end **discrimination** in their community?"*

First step: You think alone.

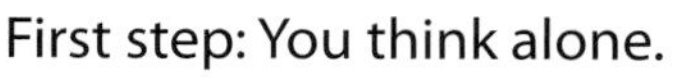

Second step: You share your ideas with a partner and come up with agreed answers.

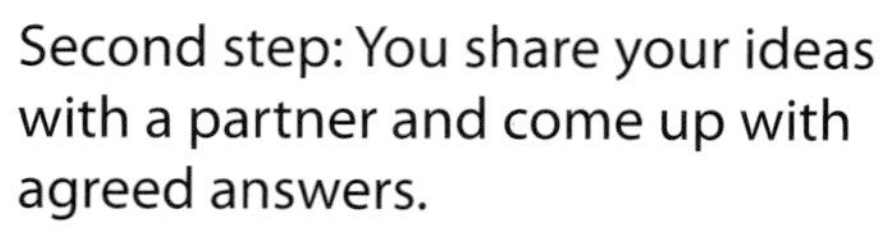

Third step: You share your ideas as a pair with another pair, making a group of four.

Final step: As a group of four you join with another group and do the same thing. You then share your ideas with the whole class!

# Christians today

TPD
Cit
PD

**Think again!**

Look quickly at the pictures below. Which people do you think are likely to be Christians?

Now look closely at each picture. Why did you think each person was or wasn't a Christian? Could you have been wrong?

What qualities do you think a Christian should have?

Do you think Christians should look different from other people?

Have you ever met someone and felt that they must be a Christian? If so, why?

Have you ever been surprised to hear someone saying they are a Christian? If so, why?

Com
TPD
Cit

Get some of the class to play the parts in the role play below.

Afterwards, talk about what the role play is saying about the attitudes of some people today.

*Narrator* – Bernie and Ash are good friends and they attend the same church. They go shopping together all the time and love to wear the latest fashions. They have arrived at church for a special prayer meeting, where they are going to pray for the homeless people in their country.

*Bernie* – (enters, crosses to chairs, talking to Ash) ... and I found this great looking pair of shoes to match the skirt perfectly.

*Ash* – (enters with Bernie, crosses to chairs) Oh, where did you find them? I can never get what I want in the shoe shops in town.

*Bernie* – Actually, it wasn't a shoe shop at all. It was a clothes shop in the new ... (taps Ash, points at Amy) Check this out.

*Amy* – (enters, wearing faded jeans and T-shirt, sits in chair, opens and reads Bible)

*Bernie* – Have you noticed how this neighbourhood seems to be going downhill?

*Ash* – I think this church should have a dress code, don't you? Excuse me, are you aware that this is a church?

*Amy* – (looks up from Bible) Excuse me?

*Ash* – I asked you if you were aware that this is a church?

*Amy* – Yes, this is a prayer meeting, isn't it? I hope I'm not in the wrong room.

*Bernie* – This is a prayer meeting, alright.

*Ash* – Do you *always* dress like *that* when you go to church?

*Amy* – I'm afraid I don't have much choice. I only have one other outfit. It's jeans and a T-shirt too.

*Bernie* – (to Ash) What did I tell you about the neighbourhood?

*Amy* – This *is* the place where we're praying for the homeless, isn't it?

*Ash* – (to Bernie) Yes, but we didn't invite any of the homeless to this meeting.

*Pat* – (enters, crosses to podium) Hi, everybody. Are we ready to pray for the homeless? Oh, I see a new face here. And you are ...?

*Amy* – My name is Amy.

*Pat* – This meeting was to *pray* for the homeless. I hope you didn't come here expecting a hand-out.

*Amy* – Oh, no. My mum has a job now and some nice people from the shelter found us a place to live. We don't need hand-outs any more.

*Pat* – You weren't thinking of coming to this church every week, were you?

*Amy* – Well, my mum has to work on Sundays, so she won't be able to make it to church here. But this was our denomination where we come from, so ...

| | |
|---|---|
| *Pat –* | How nice for you. Well, this is a prayer meeting, so I suppose we should pray for the homeless. Let's bow our heads in prayer. |
| *Pat –* | Our gracious and merciful heavenly father ... |
| *Bernie –* | Excuse me, but this just isn't working for me! |
| *Ash –* | Me neither. |
| *Pat –* | What's the problem? |
| *Bernie –* | How can I concentrate on praying, when one of us is not dressed for praying? |
| *Ash –* | It's really distracting when one of us is dressed for cleaning out the barn. |
| *Amy –* | I'm sorry, you're obviously talking about me. |
| *Bernie –* | Obviously. |
| *Amy –* | I'm sorry. I didn't mean to be a distraction. |
| *Pat –* | Listen ... what's your name again? |
| *Amy –* | Amy. |
| *Pat –* | Listen, Amy, I realise that this church is your denomination, but under the circumstances perhaps you'd be more comfortable in the community church down the road. I haven't seen a shirt and tie in that church in years. |
| *Amy –* | (stands) I'm sorry, I didn't mean to be a distraction. I ... I'll just go. (crosses toward opposite exit) |
| *Jesus –* | (enters) Amy, why are you crying? |
| *Amy –* | (startled) Who are you? |
| *Jesus –* | I'm Jesus. Jesus of Nazareth. You know me. |
| *Amy –* | Jesus! |
| *Jesus –* | You're crying because of them, aren't you? (points) |
| *Amy –* | (head down, nods silently) |
| *Jesus –* | (arm around Amy's shoulder as they exit) Don't worry about them, Amy. They won't let me in either. |

*(Based on a play by Bob Snook; http://www.fea.net/bobsnook; email: bobsnook@fea.net)*

TPD

What did Jesus mean when he said *"They won't let me in either"?*

# Faith

Com
ICT
MI
BC
TPD
SM
Cit

How has faith made an impact on people's lives?

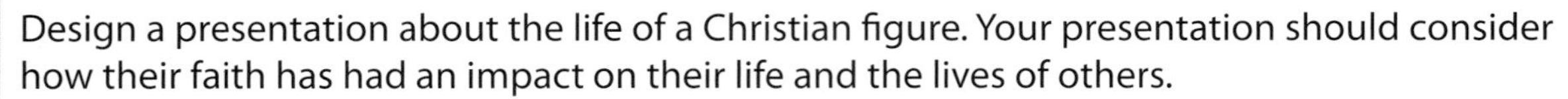

Design a presentation about the life of a Christian figure. Your presentation should consider how their faith has had an impact on their life and the lives of others.

You can choose anyone you like, but some suggestions are given below.

Your presentation should include:

- The person's life story – key life events in the order they happened
- Some quotations from or about the person
- A personal reflection on the person – what has impressed you about the impact they have made on society?
- Pictures of the person at various times in their life

Suggestions of Christian figures you could investigate:

- Dame Cicely Saunders, founder of the Hospice movement
- CS Lewis, author of *The Chronicles of Narnia*
- Saint Francis of Assisi, founder of the **Franciscan Order**
- John Calvin, a **Protestant** reformer
- Reverend John Newton, composer of the hymn 'Amazing Grace'
- Father Damien, a missionary who helped lepers
- Gordon Wilson, peace campaigner from Northern Ireland
- **Cardinal** Sin of Manila, campaigner for the poor and oppressed
- John Wesley, founder of Methodism
- Father Brian D'Arcy, author, newspaper columnist and broadcaster
- Cliff Richard, singer
- Elizabeth Fry, campaigner for prison reform
- Sir Isaac Newton, mathematician
- Robin Eames, former Church of Ireland **Archbishop** (pictured on this page)
- A local minister, priest or pastor
- A local youth leader

# Glossary

*Please note that the definitions given below relate to the work covered in this textbook. Some words may also have other alternative meanings, eg 'Diet' and 'Fast'.*

**Abolish:** To do away with or put an end to

**AIDS:** Stands for **a**cquired **i**mmune **d**eficiency **s**yndrome. AIDS is caused by a virus called HIV which attacks the body's white blood cells, meaning the body is no longer able to protect itself against disease.

**Anglican:** A member of the Church of England or a church which belongs to it. In Northern Ireland the Church of Ireland is an Anglican church.

**Apartheid:** The complete separation of races in South Africa from 1948–1994

**Apostles:** Jesus' 11 remaining disciples who were sent to preach the gospel. Paul also considered himself an apostle (1 Corinthians 15:7–10) because Jesus appeared to him and called him on the road to Damascus.

**Archbishop:** In the Church, the clergyman in charge of a large area called an archdiocese. The archbishop is in charge of the bishops.

**Arena:** The central area of a large stadium where Roman sports and gladiatorial events took place in front of an audience

**Ascension:** To ascend means to 'rise'. The Bible says that Jesus ascended to heaven 40 days after his resurrection – this is known as the Ascension.

**Atheism:** Not believing in a God or gods

**Augustinian:** Relating to Saint Augustine

**Autobiography:** A person's life story, written by that person

**Ballot:** A piece of paper on which a vote is marked in an election

**Basilica:** A special type of Catholic Church

**Bishop:** In the Church, the clergyman in charge of an area called a diocese. The bishop is in charge of the Church's activities in the diocese.

**Blaspheme:** To show disrespect for God or sacred things, usually through speech

**Boycott:** Refers to a person or group refusing to have dealings with a person or organisation, or refusing to buy a product or use a service, as a means of protest

**Canonisation:** In the Catholic Church, the process a person goes through after death in order to become a saint

**Canvass:** To try and get people to vote for you or your party, eg by going out and talking to them

**Cardinal:** A rank in the Catholic Church between archbishop and pope. Cardinals are chosen by the Pope.

**Catechism:** A series of questions and answers which explain the Christian religion; used to instruct Christians

**Chaplains:** Members of the Christian clergy who work for an institution, branch of the army, or university, etc

**Chieftains:** Leaders of areas of a land. The kingdoms in early Ireland were ruled by chieftains.

**Civil rights:** The rights of each person, upheld by the law in most countries, eg freedom of speech and freedom of movement

**Communion:** A part of some church services where bread and wine are eaten and drunk in memory of Jesus' life and death

**Compensation:** Something (often money) which is given to make up for the loss of something

**Concentration camps:** Prison camps where people were imprisoned, and in some cases tortured and killed, without any trial. The best-known concentration camps were those set up by the Nazis during the Second World War.

**Conclave:** A secret or private meeting – often refers to the meeting of cardinals for the election of a new Pope

**Confession:** The practice of admitting sins or wrongdoings

**Conspiracy:** A secret plan or plot by a group to do something

**Convert:** Someone who has changed their religion

**Corps:** (Pronounced 'core') A section of an army

**Crematorium:** A building where dead bodies are cremated. 'Cremate' means 'burn'.

**Crypt:** An underground chamber, especially beneath a church, which is often used as a burial space

**Deacon:** Someone who helped in the early Church, eg by preaching or administrative duties. Christian churches still have deacons today, but what they do depends on the denomination.

**Dermatologists:** Doctors who specialise in treating diseases and illnesses of the skin

**Diet:** A meeting of representatives

**Discrimination:** The practice of treating someone unfairly because of a prejudice against them

**Divine:** From, or to do with, God

**Druids:** Pagan priests

**Ecumenical:** Promoting the unity of the Christian Church

**Equality:** Being considered equal, and being treated equally

**Ethnic minorities:** People or groups living in an area where their race is in the minority

**Excommunication:** Being put out of the Church and its activities

**Fanatic:** Someone with extreme enthusiasm for something

**Fast:** To eat nothing or very little, often in order to concentrate on praying or some other duty

**Franciscan Order:** A reforming Order founded by Saint Francis of Assisi

**Furlough:** Leave of absence from work, often used for missionaries who go home for a while

**Gentiles:** People who are not Jewish

**Ghettos:** Slum areas of towns or cities where people belonging to a minority live

**Gospel:** Means the "Good News" of the life and teachings, death and resurrection of Jesus Christ, which leads to salvation. The four Gospels – Matthew, Mark, Luke and John – tell this story.

**Heretic:** Someone who contradicts (goes against) the teachings of the Church

**Hindu:** A member of the Hindu faith. Hinduism is the largest religion in India.

**HIV:** The virus which causes AIDS

**Holocaust:** The mass murder of Jews, gypsies, disabled people, homosexuals and others by the Nazis during the Second World War

**Holy of Holies:** The most holy place in the Jewish Temple in Jerusalem

**Holy Roman Emperor:** A king who ruled over the Holy Roman Empire

**Holy Roman Empire:** An empire in western Europe set up in AD 800. It lasted for around 1,000 years and at times included Germany, Austria, Switzerland, and parts of Italy and the Netherlands.

**Holy Spirit:** Part of the Trinity

**Honorary degree:** A degree given by a university to honour a person, even though they have not passed the exams for it

**Human rights:** The rights every person is entitled to, eg justice and freedom

**Illuminate:** To decorate a page using colours, gold or silver

**Index:** A list of books published by the Pope in 1557. It included books which Catholics were forbidden to read.

**Indulgences:** Pardons from sin granted by the Church. They could be bought from priests.

**Inequality:** Being considered unequal, and being treated unequally

**Infrastructure:** The things in place in society which allow it to work properly, eg roads, buildings, power supplies, and schools

**Interdenominational:** Involving different Christian denominations

**Intolerance:** Lack of respect for other people's beliefs and practices

**Jesuits:** Priests of the Society of Jesus. These people are dedicated to missionary work, education and helping the poor and sick.

**Kingdom:** An area ruled by a sovereign

**Local kings:** *See* chieftains

**Lutheran:** A follower of Martin Luther, or a Church which follows his beliefs

**Messiah:** The saviour that the Jewish people are waiting for. Christians believe that Jesus Christ is the Messiah.

**Minority:** A group of people who are different from most other people in an area, eg of a different race or religion

**Mixed marriages:** Marriages between people of different races or religions

**Multinationals:** Large businesses which operate in several countries

**Nonconformist:** A member of a Protestant denomination which does not 'conform' or belong to one of the main Churches, eg the Methodist Church is Nonconformist

**Order:** A religious group. People belonging to an Order take vows and devote themselves to religious aims.

**Pagan:** Someone who believes in many different gods

**Paramedical:** Refers to workers who are not doctors or nurses but are trained to give medical help

**Parkinson's disease:** A disease of the nervous system. People with Parkinson's disease find movement very difficult.

**Pentecost:** A Jewish harvest celebration. Christians believe that the Holy Spirit came to earth during Pentecost.

**Pilgrimage:** A journey to a place of religious importance

**Pope:** The head of the Catholic Church

**Prejudice:** A negative opinion about someone or something that is not based on fact

**Primitive:** Having a very basic lifestyle

**Protestants:** Members of the Protestant churches. They follow principles set up by people like Martin Luther and John Calvin during the Reformation.

**Radical:** Supporting extreme changes in society

**Reconciliation:** Bringing together opposing sides and resolving their differences

**Reformation:** A movement during the sixteenth century which began as an attempt to reform the Catholic Church, and resulted in Protestant Churches being set up

**Renaissance:** A period in European history, beginning in the fourteenth century. Great changes took place at this time in thought, culture, art and science.

**Resistance:** A secret organisation fighting for freedom in a country under enemy occupation, eg during the Second World War

**Rituals:** Acts performed as part of a religious ceremony

**Sacraments:** Outward signs of faith, eg baptism and Mass

**Sacred:** Holy and worthy of respect

**Sacrifices:** Offerings, such as animals or valuable objects, to a god

**Salvation:** Forgiveness and being let off the punishment for sin

**Salvationist:** A member of the Salvation Army

**Sanhedrin:** The main Jewish council or court in Jerusalem

**Segregate:** To separate people of different races, religions, or social classes. Segregation can take place in the workplace, schools, public transport, hospitals and even whole cities or countries.

**Seminary:** A college where priests are trained

**Slave trade:** The transportation and selling of people as slaves, especially the transportation of black Africans to Europe and North America between the sixteenth and nineteenth centuries

**Slavery:** Refers to one person owning another person and having complete control over them

**Society of Jesus:** A reforming Order founded in 1534 by Ignatius of Loyola

**Sweatshops:** Workshops where workers work long hours in poor conditions for low wages

**Ten Commandments:** Basic rules for living which the Old Testament says God gave to Moses

**Theology:** The study of religion

**Theses:** A thesis (the plural is 'theses') can refer to a principle or statement put forward by someone. The person then usually goes on to try and prove the thesis through argument.

**Trinity:** God the Father, Son and Holy Spirit – three parts to God, but one God

**Vestments:** Robes worn by a member of the clergy at religious services. These vestments will represent the position held in the Church.

**Vocation:** A calling to do a particular job

**Zealous:** Filled with intense enthusiasm

# Acknowledgements

**Acknowledgements:**
The authors and Colourpoint Books gratefully acknowledge the assistance of the following people and organisations:

The Acre Gospel Mission – especially Mission Coordinator Keith Lindsay and Dr Bill Woods OBE
Dr Alasdair McDonnell MLA
Amnesty International
The Billy Graham Evangelistic Association
Dr Brian Turner
Chichester Cathedral
The Church of Ireland
Iris Robinson MLA
Linda Colson at CCEA
The Salvation Army – especially Captains Neil and Susan McFerran; and Linda Campbell, the Regional Press Officer, Ireland
Stuart Leathem (formerly Education Officer at the Saint Patrick Centre, Downpatrick)
WEC International, especially Maud Kells
Westminster Abbey

**Picture credits:**
Getty Images: Cover (Stockbyte), 42 (left), 51, 58, 61, 68 (top), 71, 73 (left top & bottom), 75
The Dean and Chapter of Chichester Cathedral: 6
iStockphoto.com: 8, 26 (left), 80 (P_Wei)
Wesley Johnston: 13, 29, 35, 46
North Wind Picture Archives: 17, 20, 36, 44
Norman Johnston: 19, 26 (right)
Wendy Faris: 28 (right), 79 (left), 94
The Yorck Project: 30 (left)
Mary Evans Picture Library: 34 (left), 42 (right), 45
Derek Polley: 47
Iris Robinson: 48
Alasdair McDonnell: 49
Ricardo Stuckert/ABr: 50
Salvation Army: 52. 53
By kind permission of the Dean and Chapter of Westminster: 56, 63 (right), 64
Herman Hiller, New York World-Telegram & Sun: 59
O Fernandez, New York World-Telegram & Sun: 60
Corbis Images: 63 (left)
Courtesy of Billy Graham Evangelistic Association: 65, 66, 67, 69, 70
Leprosy Mission: 72 (right)
P Jaworski: 73 (top right)
Massimo Macconi: 76
Dr Bill Woods: 81, 84
Twentieth Century Fox courtesy the Kobal Collection: 86
Benny Gool: 89
John Mullen: 90
© the Representative Body of the Church of Ireland: 98

# Also in this series

Also available in this series of resources for the new Core Syllabus for Religious Education at Key Stage 3:

### Christianity in Close-up Book 1

**THE REVELATION OF GOD**

**by Wendy Faris and Heather Hamilton**

*ISBN: 978 1 904242 75 8*
*Price: £11.99*

### Christianity in Close-up Book 3

**MORALITY**

**by Juliana Gilbride and Heather Hamilton**

*ISBN: 978 1 904242 98 7*
*Price: £11.99*

In the same accessible and colourful format as Book 1, these texts include questions and activities which address the topics in a fresh and engaging style, helping to create active participation and enjoyment of the subject.

### Resource CDs

A CD of printable activity sheets and teacher resources is available for each book. These can be printed out in the necessary numbers and distributed to the class. There are also sheets specifically for teachers which provide resources for a variety of additional practical activities.

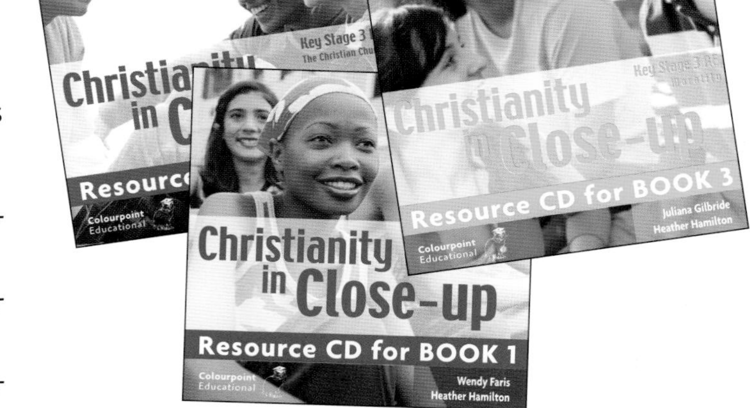


**Resource CD for Book 1**
*ISBN: 978 1 904242 85 7* *Price: £39.99 + VAT*

**Resource CD for Book 2**
*ISBN: 978 1 904242 86 4* *Price: £29.99 + VAT*

**Resource CD for Book 3**
*ISBN: 978 1 904242 99 4* *Price: £29.99 + VAT*

For a full range of materials available from Colourpoint Educational, visit our website:

**Web: www.colourpoint.co.uk**

Or contact Colourpoint Educational at:

**Tel: 028 9182 6339 Fax: 028 9182 1900**

**Email: sales@colourpoint.co.uk**

**Colourpoint Books, Colourpoint House, Jubilee Business Park, 21 Jubilee Road, Newtownards, Co Down, BT23 4YH**